I0210862

SOCIAL ETHICS:
CHRISTIAN AND NATURAL

A Problem for the Teaching Church

The Beckly Social Service Lecture

SOCIAL ETHICS:
CHRISTIAN AND NATURAL

A Problem for the Teaching Church

by

T. E. JESSOP

PROFESSOR OF PHILOSOPHY AND PSYCHOLOGY
UNIVERSITY COLLEGE OF HULL

WIPF *&* STOCK · Eugene, Oregon

Wipf and Stock Publishers
199 W 8th Ave, Suite 3
Eugene, OR 97401

Social Ethics Christian and Natural
A Problem for the Teaching Church
By Fessop, T. E.
Copyright©1952 Methodist Publishing - Epworth Press
ISBN 13: 978-1-5326-3060-6
Publication date 4/6/2017
Previously published by Epworth Press, 1952

Every effort has been made to trace the current copyright
owner of this publication but without success. If you have
any information or interest in the copyright, please contact the publishers.

PREFACE

THESE pages are an expansion of the Social Service Lecture delivered before the Conference of the Methodist Church at Preston in July 1952. Being a child and continuing member of this Church, I am specially sensitive of the privilege of being called into the succession of Beckly Lecturers, and can pay to the late Mr J. H. Beckly, whose endowment created it, a more than formal tribute.

The purpose of the Lecture, it is laid down, is to 'set forth the social implications of Christianity, and to further the development of a Christian sociology, and the expression of the Christian attitude in reference to social, industrial, economic, and international subjects'. That is a wide enough field to move in, and it has not by any means been over-explored. The journey I have taken begins with a quick analysis of the Church's unhappy position in a secularized society, which leads me to suggest the urgency of a campaign to educate Christians in what they stand for, in the Faith in general and in social doctrine in particular. When, however, I look round for a social doctrine designed to cover the problems distinctive of our day, I fail to find one, and conclude that we are trying to judge the actions of organized groups, and our own actions when we are functioning as members of such groups, entirely by moral rules that were framed for the relations of individuals in their individual capacity; in other words, that we are thinking with an individual ethic about matters that call for a social ethic. All that follows is an attempt to emphasize this distinction, by indicating some of the confusions that arise through our ignoring it, and some of the clarifications it can bring into our thinking about social problems in their present form. Our actual thinking, I urge, is much too abstract, inadequate to the complexity of both moral relations and facts. Accordingly, I have had to offer illustrations of concrete thinking, with which the little book ends. Throughout I have aimed at being readable by anyone who can hold his mind to a problem, and have therefore ruthlessly excluded the paraphernalia of erudition.

This is but an essay, incomplete, tentative—indeed, fumbling. I would ask for more attention to its outlook and technique or method than to its details, for the former come from me as a moral philosopher, which I am by profession, whereas the latter come from me as a moralist, which I am by conceit.

CONTENTS

ONE

THE SOCIAL INEFFECTIVENESS OF THE CHURCH

THAT the Church (or Churches, if you will) is not having its due impact on society is evident from the gross fact that the general tendency of society in its organized forms —as State, trade unions, professional associations—is to pursue its affairs without any reference to the religious view of man. Not that society is becoming pagan, for this would mean that it is falling back on a primitive sort of religion. It is becoming secular, that is, either explicitly repudiating or simply ignoring all religion whatever in the shaping of its aims and programmes; which is a quite new thing in the career of the race, and consequently deeply disconcerting to those of us who believe that in this respect the race has not been wrong. True, society is now moralizing patches that had been left unmoralized (it has done that sort of thing often before), in particular placing its total resources at the disposal of all instead of reserving most of them for a very small minority. But it neither gives nor feels any religious reasons for such betterments.

Well, it may be said, does the absence of such reasons matter so long as the good things are done? Of course it matters. The way in which we do things is deeply affected by our reasons for doing them. For example, the secularism of the current movement for social justice has in it a great deal of hate, deliberately and resourcefully fostered, and hate works by lying propaganda and shock-methods, and perverts justice from fairness for all into class-greed—the bottom dog fighting to become top dog. A Christian reason would condemn that, in whatever class the hate and greed may lie. Further, the natural consequences of action without the religious reason are different from those of action with it. The secular outlook is short, and therefore isolates problems that are not really isolable, and in its purblind concentration on the immediate or fashionable problems hurries to a solution of them that creates other, and perhaps worse, problems, and by the neglect of old problems aggravates these. Recently we have dealt with the distribution of wealth in a way that has impaired the production of it; we have neglected general moralization, and are therefore being faced with a swelling, at once disgusting and expensive, of divorce and crime; in making public office more easily got, we have multiplied public corruption; and the encouragement of hate and hurry is leading us to undo with our left hand the efforts after peace which we are making with our right. There *is* need of Christian motives, of the long-range Christian outlook and of the Christian sense of the unity or wholeness of life.

The Church, then, has been shelved, is no longer an important controlling force. But should it be such a force? Why complain or lament if it has no power in an alien field? Are politics and economics really within its province? At once we are faced with a question of doctrine, a basic issue on which I must take sides if I am to proceed to a positive discussion of Christian social education. I shall have to indicate, however sketchily, my reasons for rejecting an old, and in some quarters still-continuing, contention that the Church has no direct concern with the structure and movement of earthly society. Three arguments that have been put forward within the Church for this contention may be mentioned. (*a*) The Christ was not a social reformer, and the Kingdom He founded is

not a happy, prosperous, and just State, but a spiritual
fellowship aiming at a perfection that is not realizable on
earth. (*b*) The whole order of space and time is transient,
incapable of embodying any eternal values, and, moreover, full of enticements to chain our affections to it.
Consequently, the Christian must sit lightly in it, taking
none of its affairs at all seriously, but fixing his interest
on the matters that belong, not to his or anybody else's
present stability and happiness, but to ultimate salvation.
Love of anything created is a sin; we are called to contempt of the world. (*c*) A God who is Father is concerned
with His children individually, and it is only one by one
that we can be saved. Religion is a personal affair, the
most personal of all, a direct link between the finite
immortal soul and the greater Soul that made it. Society
is, of course, a natural state of man, but all that is religiously relevant in it is the mesh of personal relations
between individual and individual, not its group-aspects.

For each of these views supporting texts can be found in
Scripture, and each of them has an echo and a warrant in
the best Christian experience of the past and present.
Yet they are heresies if we may say, as the books sometimes do, that a heresy is usually right in what it affirms,
but wrong in what it denies—that is, wrong in adding
'only' to its affirmations. Let us glance correctingly at
them in turn.

(*a*) The tendency to reduce our Lord to a social
reformer was the most serious error of one of the phases of
'Liberal Christianity'. It was an error in three ways—a
plain misreading of the Gospels, a contradiction of the
universal doctrine of the Church, and a denial or ignoring
of the impression made by Jesus on the souls of a vast
cloud of witnesses. It is biblically, theologically, and
experientially false. Social reform, in the sense of the
public changing of public institutions, was the very thing

that He most plainly avoided. Does it follow, however, that His followers must do the same? Only on either of two assumptions: that that avoidance was intended as an example for us to copy, and not something bound up with the uniqueness of His person and work, or that the immense difference between the simple life of perhaps a million Jews two thousand years ago and the complexly organized life of the teeming millions of an industrialized Western society of today requires no difference in our Christian range and methods. The first assumption shocks my religious sensibility, the second my reason.

(*b*) That this world and its values are not the most important of all things is obviously an essential part of the Christian position. Compared with God and the life of spirits in His presence they are indeed contemptible. But this contrast is not the summary of the Christian position: it leaves too much out. The world, we hold, came from God; and, we also hold, we were set in it by Him; and some values—health and happiness—follow from its nature and ours. This life, we hold, is a testing ground for another life; some of its commissions and omissions, even in worldly relations, have eternal consequences. The Son of God, we yet further hold, entered this world and life for a while, so consecrating it—and not solemnly only, but also by noticing and appreciating even the little spring flowers in it, and the short-lived sparrows making merry on the flat house-tops. So believing, we cannot damn wholemindedly this terrestrial theatre and all that is played out in it. To do so would be blasphemy. This world of space and time is only relatively, not absolutely, unimportant, that is, as compared with heaven; and it is also relatively important, that is, as divinely ordained, divinely visited, still divinely indwelt, and the way to heaven or to hell.

(*c*) The emphasis on personal relations goes back, the

biblical scholars tell us, to Jeremiah and Ezekiel, indeed to Hosea, and to say that Jesus endorsed it is not merely true, but an understatement. But the very fact that the ideal He set us was that all relations should be personal is one of the reasons why we cannot watch without concern, indeed without resistance, the monstrous growth of impersonal organization and remote control. To say that this is not a religious concern and then retire to our devotions and friendships, which plainly are, is to throw up the sponge, to abandon an enlarging aspect of modern life as beyond the sphere of redemption, or even of mending. The living together of millions, especially when they have an elaborate economy and culture, necessitates organization. The easy way—now being followed—is to multiply this and try to make it work by its own momentum. The Christian way is to have it run not by inexorable ordinances of State, but by persons who can be trusted to act for persons; and further—this being a truth *within* the third heresy—by so changing the individuals of the group that some kinds or degrees of organization become unnecessary, such as those due to wickedness, which calls for evangelization, and those due to stupidity and ignorance, which, nearly as bad in effect, call for education.

All this arguing, however, has a touch of pedantry in it. After all, is not a Christian one who, in the love of God that has redeemed him, loves his fellows? And who that really does this can look inactively on poverty and sickness, or simply watch old folk shiver because their children put cars and wireless sets before even the bond of nature, or bear to see children inadequately educated and then turned out into a diseducating environment? Until recently Christians *could* do (even if they didn't) individually for such human casualties nearly all that needed to be done, and there is still room for little individual services, and also for voluntary co-operative efforts: but much contemporary misfortune and moral evil are bound up with conditions that can only be changed, or changed quickly, by political decision, and also by public resources, since the material means of help, being now larger and more scientific (e.g. for sickness), have become too expensive for individuals to provide, and rules and regulations further limit individual action. To say, then, that Christianity has nothing to do with politics and economics is to construe these terms abstractly, forgetting that they stand for the means by which health and wealth and even social morality are nowadays to a large extent controlled.

The Church ought, then, to be interested—in the strong sense of effectively influencing—the various social institutions and processes by which a great part of our lives is now being shaped. Why, then, is it so ineffective? Partly because of such misgivings and hesitations as are reflected in those contentions which I have impudently called heresies: but these are less uttered than they used to be. Partly also because of the sensible recognition that it would in practice be impossible and in doctrine undesirable for the Church to set up a political band-wagon of its own—in practice because the secular party-differences are as strong among the members of the Church as among those outside, and in doctrine because the authority of the Church is confined to the general religious and moral principles of living, not extending to the particular causal means by which those principles are to be applied to a given society at a given time (e.g. we cannot worthily drag in the name of God to sanctify either the nationalization of an industry or opposition to this). Further, some of the social changes distinctive of our time have made it impossible for the Church to exercise its social influence in the old way. I am thinking chiefly of changes of temper. For example, there is the current repudiation of discipline—one of our fashionable hypocrisies, for much of it is only touchiness (the pettiest form of pride) masquerading as moral respect for freedom or equality. There is also the overswollen demand for pleasure, mostly in its passive forms, making the provision of it one of our major industries: the voice of the Church can scarcely reach entertainment-drugged minds, and if it could would be scarcely intelligible: this being but one instance of the filling of our environment with more and more allurements, enabling a mind empty within to exist by stimulation from without, and making the Church, formerly unmissable among the few social institutions, hardly discernible or audible amid the many and noisy voices that force themselves on our attention today. Lastly— for it is enough to be suggestive, not exhaustive—the landslide from the Church which the concurrent tendencies of our industrialized society have brought about, has heavily depleted the Church's resources of personnel and of material wealth, and thereby restricted the scale and pertinacity of some of its activities.

My purpose is not to attach blame. The Church is caught up in a human torrent that seems to be passing beyond human control. The instruments of applied science, and the new mass-determination of politics, marked by powerful caprice, have combined to produce a waxing speed of movement and an enlarging complexity of organization that make it naturally harder for the Church to make itself heard and felt. There is, of course, blame somewhere for all this, but it is distributed throughout society and through the generations, and of it the Church must take its share, though no more. Ignoring this question of blame, what I have been trying to do so far is to call for an explicit and frank recognition of a fact— that in the matter of guiding society the Church has lost its grip; and of a duty—that under modern conditions the Church is obliged to add to its indefeasible task of saving individual souls a practical concern with the public programmes, laws, administration, and suchlike, within which individuals now have to live, and which make it either easier or harder—excepting always the incalculable grace of God—for individuals to be saved.

The practical question is how this duty is to be discharged. It would be silly of me to dare to attempt to give the whole answer, and it would be rash of me to claim to give the whole of even one part of the answer. My experience, like everybody else's, is very limited, and my training, like most people's, has been specialized. I am a teacher. I shall therefore consider the problem of the Church's social ineffectiveness so far only as it is an educational one. My plea is to be that in this field of reference the Church should resume, or assume more fully, its teaching office.

This plea may, indeed, be taken quite generally, that is, regarding the Faith in all its aspects, since in this matter the present position is astonishing. Nearly all the lay members of the Church (I am still using this term compendiously for the Churches) have very little understanding, or even rote-memory, of what the Faith is. A football fan knows more about football than most Christians know about Christianity. This is a hard saying, but it must be said. Ask most of our members what they believe, and after not many sentences they would be finished, and for lack of substance, not of mere words. A practising member of a political party, or an atheist, or a bright young thing who has read a popular book or two on science, would make rings round them, stump them, and perhaps leave them unsure. They probably know quite a lot about their job and about some hobby, but it has not occurred to them to get to know much about the Faith, or, if it has, they have shirked the bother, or else they have naïvely supposed that there really isn't much to know about it. The faith they have is in a little Faith. They have no idea of the immense content of Christianity, and therefore miss its immense grip on the imagination and emotions, which makes worship spontaneous and magnificent, and its immense grip on the will, which makes conduct untiringly and lastingly Christian. This poverty of belief underlies, I am sure, much of the rest of our poverty, and is thus one of the chief single causes of our ineffectiveness.

What is the reason? Surely, in part and in large part, lack of teaching. The religious instruction which people received as children (some received none) had to be accommodated to their tender understanding and sensibilities: it covered nothing like the whole Faith, and what was given had to be served as milk, not as meat. This was paedagogically right. But after childhood most people have received no further religious instruction—in any definite sense of this term—and many of them, criticizing their childish religion from an adult point of view, reject it without considering whether there is an adult form of Christian belief and practice to take its place. In this way we have lost many members and failed to get many. Those who, by the providence of God, do both enter the Church and remain in it grow emotionally and volitionally rather than in understanding; that is, they advance but little in range and quality of religious *belief*. We have no plan, no regular method of either inducement or discipline, to ensure or make probable such advancement. It almost seems as if our chief evangelical concern were only to get people into the Church, then leaving them to its traditional routine; which is specially unfortunate when, as very often happens, many are admitted without preliminary instruction. There are, of course, exceptions, usually due to the initiative of individual ministers, conducting really educative classes or punctuating their preaching with teaching sermons.

This is not to require every member to be a theologian or a biblical scholar. I am insisting on the fact that the great majority of the churchgoers, and even of the church-members, of today are unable, beyond a few vague sentences, to tell outsiders what they stand for. And this fact, I assume, is dreadful. One of our most urgent requirements is therefore an organized drive in adult religious education. If it be objected that the Church was doing very well fifty years ago without anything of the kind, I would reply first, that there *was* something of the kind (e.g. expository preaching, regular Bible classes), and secondly, that members then had the habit of private Bible-reading, which consisted, moreover, not in pecking at a dozen verses set for them as a task, but in finding their own way about the great Book and eating the very heart out of it, and that through this loving and strenuous labour they got a much more deeply educated mind than many of us get under our present elaborate and expensive school system. By the way, they spoke better, simpler English, for it was good English that they were there regularly reading, not the fluffy, floppy, floundering wish-wash that passes as speech today.

There I have gone beyond my reference; but it was necessary to set my theme against that larger background, from which it is inseparable. One part of that wide ignorance of Christian doctrine is ignorance of its bearing on contemporary social problems, on the matters that vex and perplex us in our *group*-life. That bearing does not become evident to us by the light of nature; it has to be taught; and we are not teaching it, or are not teaching it enough. In consequence, most Christians are as confused and baffled by the contemporary situation, and therefore as ineffective in it, as the people who have no connexion with the Church; which is a very poor advertisement of Christianity. Those outside have noticed this, and have written us off, some of them with regret, some with contempt. This is the result that bothers me, and that sets me my theme.

It may seem as though that is all that needs to be said— the harsh definition of the situation, and the drawing of the moral. If so, we can leave all argument behind and concentrate on the practical, clinching conclusion, which calls for nothing less than outright decision, that we must now go ahead with the teaching drive. The matter is not so simple. We are not ready to go ahead. But has not every major Church in our country a special department for training and action with regard to social affairs? Yes; such departments have been one of the good consequences of the miserable aftermath of the first World War. But they have not had the support they require. It is much too easy to tell them to go ahead if we are not prepared to go with them. Even so, granted that we have the appropriate institutions and that we are willing to help them with moral and financial support, the problem is not yet solved even on paper. A large and sustained drive would set us the question of organization—for example, finding the teachers and training *them*. With that, however, I cannot deal. My concern in the following pages is with a prior question, one at a deeper level—namely, *what are we to teach?*

The question will seem stupid, since the answer is on the surface of all that I have been saying—namely, the Christian doctrine of society. The trouble is that there isn't one, or, to speak more precisely, that we have not formulated it and drawn out its implications for the peculiar society of our day. The lack has been observed, and the contrast drawn between us and the Communists, who, claiming like us to have a general philosophy of life, have also brought out of it particular, concrete, topical conclusions, know just what sort of social order they want, and are working with all their resources—the chief of which is resourcefulness—to get it. The contrast is not, of course, quite fair, since Communism is the wholly secular programme of a political party, is earthy and particular and topical for this reason; and Communists get things done because in their planning and doing they are entirely untrammelled by moral scruple, the repudiation of the whole corpus of European ethics (Greek and Roman as well as Christian) as '*bourgeois*' being an integral part of their philosophy. Nevertheless, the contrast has some point: although we Christians, as Christians, have no authority to draw up a blue-print and cajole for votes on it, we have not made clear to ourselves and to others the main principles that should govern the life of a twentieth-century society. True, we have talked of peace, justice, liberty, and brotherhood, but we have scarcely given either skeleton or life to these vague abstractions.

There *has been* a Christian doctrine of society. There was one in the Middle Ages, when the Church was the sole stable governing agency in Western Europe. It was admirable; it deserves still to be studied; but it was admirable for its time, and would need expansion and correction in the light of our vastly changed circumstances. One illustration will suffice to rob this statement of abstractness and dogmatism. The medieval Church condemned usury, which then meant interest, not exorbitant interest only. In so doing, by the way, they were primarily and consciously following not Jesus (Luke 6³⁵ is not specific in the Vulgate), but Aristotle, though they certainly added the Christian overtone of love. They were thinking of simple individual transactions. In those days an ordinary man kept his wealth in his chest. If he lent a part of it, he lost nothing, provided he got back all that he lent. Therefore he had no ground for charging interest: to do so would have been to exploit the needy—for at that time, in the simple transactions envisaged, only the needy borrowed. Distress, the Church rightly judged, cannot be made the occasion of profit. But in modern times a man keeps his liquid wealth in a bank, and gets interest on it while it is there. If, therefore, he lends, he loses interest, and is entitled, by the principle of justice (which a man of charity may suspend), to recoup it. Further, the great majority of modern borrowers are not in distress, but seek money in order to make more money with it. Industry would perish without credit. The circumstances being very different, the moral judgement has to be. In other words, 'usury' in the Middle Ages and 'usury' now do not in fact mean the same thing. But the underlying principle, the condemnation of the exploitation of misfortune of estate, remains valid.

There was another Christian doctrine of society in Calvin. I am not sure that *it* was admirable, at any rate as he applied it in Geneva. But, again, we live under different conditions, which, if we are to surmount them in a Christian way, require us both to think out new ways of applying old principles and to find further principles for situations so novel (e.g. industrial strikes) that the old principles alone have no obviously adequate application to them and send us on circuitous lines of inference which ordinary people distrust. During the last thirty years or so there have been a number of attempts to build up a body of principles adapted to present-day needs. If this were a full-length book, I should be almost obliged to review them and gratefully use their insights. None of them, however, has won wide approval. If I say that I find such of them as I have from time to time read either too remote from actualities or biased in a particular ecclesiastical or party-political direction, I do so not to disparage them, but to underline the difficulty of the enterprise. Further, I am doubtful whether they could be put into a form that would make them teachable to the generality of church members. We *are*, then, without an up-to-date and generally teachable Christian doctrine of society.

TWO

THE THEOLOGICAL DOCTRINE OF SOCIETY

THERE is an indispensable role for a very general religious doctrine of society, one that has no particular place or time in view but holds of society everywhere and anywhere. We get such a doctrine when, instead of reflecting on the facts of the here and now and the problems they set, we go straight to the root of the Faith and dig out of it its immediate social implications. These will contain no detail, i.e. no detail is logically deducible from the Faith—yet they will cover, in the sense of applying to, a vast amount of detail in a sweeping way. We shall get a doctrine of society that is theological in the strict sense of being based entirely on the idea of God.

I shall assume that a religion is not anything with something called God in it, but an outlook and attitude that is God-centred. It is all too easy to relax this firm requirement. Even evangelicalism, for instance, is in danger of slipping away from it, for, so far as it heavily emphasizes man's need, it is near to being man-centred: it is always in theological peril of *reducing* God to a Saviour. Similarly, the so-called 'social gospel' tends to make a society's plight, or its ambition, the centre of reference, and thereby to *reduce* God to a *Deus ex machina*, a miraculous reformer or a mighty national ally. It is one of the most important uses of theology—for which laymen have too easy a contempt—to warn us against such unintentionally impious distortions, due to obsession with practical urgencies, of the idea and place of God. Nothing can fairly be called God that does not possess two marks—(*a*) being supreme in the universe, and (*b*) being capable of entering into personal relations with us, who are persons in His universe, for there is no ground for giving the divine name to a mere force, if such were supposed to be the ultimate factor. The second mark requires a being that is itself a person. *At least* a person, theologians might wish to add; possibly something higher, if that be conceivable by us (which it isn't), but certainly not anything lower. The two marks together give us a Sovereign, a Supreme Person.

Religion, then, is minimally belief in a Sovereign Person. This is the ground of worship in the sense of aweful adoration. It is the continuing Old Testament notion in our Faith. When we grasp it firmly, it holds us back from that impudent familiarity which we may slide into when we bring in the notion of Father not to enrich the Jewish idea of God but to displace it. It is also the rock-bottom ground of a religious man's obedience. To admit that there is a Supreme Being is to admit that everything and everyone is under that Being; and to admit that that Being is a person implies that *our* subjection takes the form of obedience, since this is possible only by a person and toward a person. We do, indeed, say that the sun, the planets, the stars, the winds, and so on, 'obey' the laws of Nature; but this is a very loose figure of speech. They obey nothing, not even God, since they can neither apprehend nor voluntarily·respond to any command. God rules them not by giving them orders or making appeals, but by so making them that they cannot help doing what they are doing. This is plainly not obeying, not conscious conformity with a detected rule or ideal. The sun and the stars and suchlike are in a *merely* creaturely relation to God, acting inevitably as they do because God framed them to act in that way. We humans, on the contrary, are in a personal relation to Him, able to learn His will, able also, within limits (some at least of which grace overcomes), to respond, and under obligation to respond.

If so much be clear, we may now draw out the primary social implication of religion. Since religion *means* belief in a Supreme Person, and since this *means* that nothing whatever is exempt from His sovereignty, it follows that *societies as well as individuals are under the divine jurisdiction.* This may be called the first article of the religious doctrine of society. Being deduced from the minimal content of the idea of God, there is nothing distinctively Christian about it; it is part and parcel of the theistic position. Christianity shares it with, for instance, Judaism and Islam.

Abstract though this article appears to be, it is not remote from life. It has a plainly practical reference. A people gets some guidance merely from knowing whose authority it is under. How concrete the article can be made is instanced by the ancient Jews, for whom the laws in the Old Testament, conceived as the laws of God, formed the bulk of the laws of their land, and regulated the rest; and by the present Moslem nations, whose basic body of law, principles and details alike, is taken from the Koran.

In Christendom there can be nothing comparable to these two systems, in which the distinction of sacred law and secular law scarcely arises. For Christianity is not a religion of law. Its Founder did not leave behind a corpus of regulations for the detailed government of either corporate or individual conduct, but instead, reaching down to a deeper level, made the harder requirement of an ever-developing conscience guided by the utterly general principle of 'love' and assisted by grace. He believed that mankind had grown up enough to be promoted from the childish following of rigid rules to the intelligent and sensitive application of a principle. For us

Christians, therefore, the fundamental article means that a society shall seek in each and all of its decisions and doings to know and obey the will of God for the matter in hand, that the policy, ordinances and actions of a society shall be made as consistent with the divine purpose as that society's knowledge, practical intelligence, moral insight and executive power allow of. And, we are promised, a society so striving will be given a supernatural increment of wisdom and strength.

Our article is not one of the true but useless things. Take it as a *criterion* and bring it to bear on our current democracy. Its relevance at once becomes evident. It indicts one of the most general and distinctive tendencies in our national practice—namely, the way in which the idea of political sovereignty is in fact being worked out. It has to indict that way because that way is entirely secular. Do we not now assume, as a matter of course, that a nation *ought* to be master of its own house, lord of its own affairs, in the sense that its rulers do no more than exercise an authority delegated to them by the people, and therefore are responsible only to the people? Of course, this is democracy. But it used to be held, in its fighting days in this country, with religious qualifications that modified it deeply, e.g. that all of us are responsible to God. By now this religious reference has been almost entirely wiped out. Not that we are simply, shyly, healthfully reticent about it, reluctant to drag the sacred name into the hurly-burly of politics, but that we have either ignored or repudiated the divine authority.

The way in which this fashionable secularity most patently shows itself is in the meaning we give to law and the manner in which we make law. A law now means in theory what the constitutionally represented majority insist on, and in fact it is what the most powerful pressure-group manages to get through Parliament. The difference between theory and practice is in the present context irrelevant, for religiously both the theory and the practice stand condemned, since both alike mean that law is what *we*—some group or other of humans—*want* or *will*, not what we believe, after genuine inquiry, to be as near to God's will as our insight can make it and the circumstances allow. There is not the slightest effort nowadays to ascertain God's will in such a matter. It doesn't even occur to us to bring God in at all. So-and-so is what we want, and *therefore* we propagandize, press, wire-pull, and vote for it until we get it. After all, people would say when challenged, isn't this just what is meant by the sovereignty of the people? True, we have dropped the near-blasphemy, *vox populi vox Dei*, but only because the saying has lost all meaning after we have either dismissed God from political reference or denied His very existence. Democracy is fast becoming *merely* a majority seeking and getting its own way. This is the only alternative we can now think of to despotism by a minority, which we very properly abhor. That we can only think of two extremes is a proof of the poverty of our political imagination as well as of our religious understanding.

But we do, in our demand for this law and that, at least have some regard for the morally right? To some extent, certainly, but this note is declining, except in so far as this or that section demands what is right for itself, rather than that impartial right which proves its impartiality by giving as well as claiming; and, anyhow, it is hard to discern in the talk of the street, in the vulgarity of propaganda, and in the spiteful squabbles of council chambers and Parliament, any determined care to find out what the right is. The level of debate has slumped, and naturally, for we address one another only, frankly presupposing that the whole business of politics is our own affair. The sovereignty of God over *society* is a lost idea.

So much for the indicting application of the first social article. As a *positive, guiding principle* the article is again illuminating. If in the shaping of law and in all other social deeds we remembered that herein we are all under a higher jurisdiction, that political sovereignty is itself subject to divine sovereignty, we should not, indeed, be able by an easy bit of reasoning to deduce just what we should do, since this must be learned from the study of particular facts and of the general causal connexion of facts. Religion is not a substitute for effortful inquiry. But it is a high stimulus to it; and it greatly improves inquiry, for when we see ourselves under God, self-reference is diminished, our perspective is vastly extended, remote as well as near consequences are reviewed, and we take especial care with our moral principles, both to conceive them rightly and to apply them rightly. Who, or who that acknowledges God, can deny that under this high responsibility and with that large vision we would approximate our wills and ways to the divine way, and in so doing inevitably fashion a better society?

That a nation, even a sovereign nation, indeed a democratic nation, is just as much under the sovereignty of God as the individual is, is clearly a useful, practical, improving truth, not a merely theoretical one, and as it comes straight from the root of religion, being an immediate implicate of the idea of God, it may be laid down as the founding article of the religious doctrine of society.

Among the meanings implicit within it is one that deserves to be drawn out and stated separately as a second article—namely, that *the aims, structures, and processes of society must be made compatible with God's will for the individual*, which is his salvation. In other words (passing over the various interpretations of 'salvation'), society must so organize the external environment, taking this to include the cultural as well as the material factors, as at least not to hinder, and so far as possible to favour, the full flowering of our spiritual possibilities.

Although this holds of every secular society—a club, a trade union, a political party, a municipality—I shall chiefly have in mind a nation. The article neither says nor implies that a nation must do the work of the Church. The Church is a wholly religious fellowship, existing to maintain the worship of God, to guard, refine and develop the inexhaustible content of the Faith, and to pray and toil for the salvation of all individuals in all nations. It has to be understood entirely in religious terms, although, as I noted in the first chapter, it cannot tear religion out of the common things of life. A nation, however, considered in its organized aspect as the State, is directly responsible for these common things. It has to ensure the provision of food, health, communications, internal order, defence, justice, and education; or, to express this more generally, it has to frame as much of the machinery of a nation's living as requires the consent and resources of the nation as a whole. This definition precludes the State from being directly concerned with salvation. If it were, it would become an intolerable busybody, a monstrous Inquisition, a totalitarian despot. For a State has to be coercive, and it is to enable it to be so that it is given the whole nation's resources: armed with these it is irresistible by individuals. Such an organization *cannot* bring about salvation (but only a visible caricature of it), and therefore ought not to try. That office has to be entrusted to a body appropriately formed and informed, and in particular incapable of coercion. When either body, State or Church, usurps the functions of the other, it distorts them.

Granted that State and Church have each their proper sphere, we have to interpret the second article accordingly —that is, with a limitation, not so reading it as to turn the State into an instrument of the Church. It is not the business of the State to make us Christians; indeed, it cannot, being able at most to make us look like Christians when we are in public. What the State has to do is to lay out the conditions under its power in such a way that these conditions shall not be opposed to, but rather facilitate, our becoming Christians. Although it is not to try to save us, it has to bear in mind that we are salvable. More bluntly, in all its arrangements for us it must never regard us as merely hands for work, bodies to be kept well, and minds to be trained in useful skills, but should remember that we are immortal souls.

The sheer weight and complexity of administrative machinery, and the contemporary speeding up of social change, tend to push this religious requirement out of sight. It is less bothersome to let the machinery work by its own momentum, and to handle each new problem in the light of its most obvious or urgent features. So far as overburdened politicians rule a people in that manner, they forget the immortal destiny of the citizens, and their own as well; and so far as we citizens are responsible for piling burden after burden upon them, we are to blame for the resultant foreshortening of outlook and mechanization of method. I doubt if our second article can be met until politicians are given less to do instead of more. They have no leisure to study what is likely to be the effect of their actions on men's souls. The wonder is that some of them nevertheless do. These are men of exceptional stature, and their number is diminishing.

Over a large range of its activities, a Government can put obstacles in the way of our spiritual awakening and maturing. In some countries this has been done wittingly; in most it happens unwittingly, under the pressure of events, or under pressure from the citizens. In a democracy it is the body of citizens rather than the Government that is chiefly responsible for the breaking of the second article. This may be quite simply illustrated, with special reference to current conditions, in three respects: (a) The expansion of applied science has made possible a spectacular production of wealth. This is one of the largest (in the literal sense) pieces of advance that man has made during the last hundred years or so. The process itself is exciting, and the products of it have ringed us round with amenities. But the process has become so vast and time-absorbing, and the products have so much come to be felt as necessaries, making us want more and more of them, that we now think of ourselves chiefly as producers and consumers. The economic aspect of life has become so obtrusive, dominating even politics, that it is thrusting other aspects into the background. To the extent to which this is happening—and it has gone fearfully far—we are seeking an end, and employing means, that are incompatible with our spiritual unfolding. (b) Outside of work we now expect a round of pleasure, and pleasure not created by ourselves, but provided for us, so that the provision of pleasure is now very many men's work. This has gone so far that we are being drugged instead of refreshed by entertainment. One of our healthy needs is being turned into an obsessive pursuit, into a lust, and a great deal of the entertainment supplied to us is deliberately devised to make and keep us lustful, in both the general and the special senses of this term. In consequence, we are not leaving ourselves leisure for the cultivation of the soul, and at the same time we are making the soul less and less able to be cultivated. (c) These two obsessions have coarsened our minds to such a degree that we unashamedly allow ourselves vulgarities and immoralities that have already begun to undermine public decency: dishonesty, for example, is being more and more accepted in high places and low, and sexual infidelity has ceased to be socially disgraceful. Youngsters are growing up in this atmosphere and with these examples. In many walks of life it requires something approaching heroism to think straight and walk straight.

In these three ways, which are but samples, our nation is building up a set of practices and standards that militate against any natural opening of the soul.

Now the next step. A society hasn't a soul. Only individuals have souls. A society is not immortal; it has merely a history with an end sooner or later. Only individuals outlast the disappearance of history, and only they can be summoned thereafter to give an account of their doings. From the religious point of view, therefore, individuals are much more important than societies. Despite the fashion of the day, I can see no escape from this conclusion, unless I repudiate theology; and none from an implicate of it, which may be formulated as the third constitutive article of the religious doctrine of society —namely, that *individuals cannot be required to exist wholly for society* (here again 'society' means any group, from the family to the State). Anything that has a soul cannot be tied down completely to anything that exists only in history—that is, in the order of space and time.

The least obvious bearing of this may be indicated first. The article excludes a very common interpretation of human history. Take an analogy. Biologically, each living creature completes its function, we are told, when it contributes to the perpetuation of its species. Now enlarge and idealize this notion, bringing in the motive of conscious altruism. We then get the idea that each human generation, besides producing the next, must live for it, and the next must do the same, and so on, the generations thus building up a growing volume and excellence of achievement which the final generation, before it is wiped out by some astronomical catastrophe, will inherit and enjoy in a brief blaze of glory. It is in this sense that we usually understand 'the far-off divine event to which creation moves'. But that is morally shocking, for it makes every individual and every generation except the last morally instrumental to the last—which is altruism *à outrance*, making the very meaning or value of the existence of the overwhelming majority of humans consist in their service to an ultimate favoured generation. It is also theologically shocking, because it binds man wholly to the present order, finding the meaning of history wholly within history; and also because it forces us to think of men most importantly in groups (in generations). It may be right, but if it is, some of our steadiest moral instincts are wrong, and religion is wrong—and outside *any* religious view it is plain nonsense; so that if it is right, everything else is wrong, which is proof enough that *it* is wrong. Anyhow, what a theistic religion posits is a realm of being beyond space and time into which the individual survives and for which he exists and in which he completes his destiny.

The most obvious bearing of the third article is that it sets a limit to the claims of a group on its members, and to the loyalty of members to the group. We must beware of falling into the present fashion of using the article simply as the religious repudiation of totalitarianism, whether this be benevolent or otherwise. Society means any group of mentally interacting humans, and the doctrine means that no society of any kind (except possibly the Church, if this were on earth all that it ought to be) has a claim to my whole or supreme loyalty. Not even my family. We have many loyalties. Sometimes they clash; they are bound to do so in a sinful world. In such an event we have to sort them out in an order of importance, which is at times an agonizing business (and therefore often shirked). But what the supreme loyalty is for the religious man is in principle quite clear to him: it is to

c

God. Admittedly, it is sometimes clear in principle only, as when our loyalty to God has to be shown through service to certain of our fellows and we don't know which of them has the overriding claim. It is utterly clear when a directly religious issue is at stake, as when a religious man is commanded or tempted to abjure his creed, stop his devotions, or go against his conscience.

The article is deduced from theism in its general form. In Christian theism the emphasis on the individual is specially strong. Our Lord spoke, indeed, to crowds, but not as crowds; His words were clearly addressed to each individual in them. Some of his most revealing contacts were with individuals—for example, with Nicodemus, the Samaritan woman, the Pharisee-host who omitted to wash his feet, and the woman who repaired the omission by raining her tears over them; and His most appealing parables are about individuals. He certainly loved His nation, so much so that at the end He wept over its degenerate capital, but it was far less to Jewry that He spoke than to Jews held in mind one by one. God's concern for us singly is so dominant a note of the Master's message that He even generalized it, perhaps not poetically only, to bring in the sparrow as well as the man. To all which may be added that His own coming set the highest seal on His valuation of the human individual. God chose as the means of His final self-revealing nothing so impersonal as a brightening or darkening of the face of Nature, or as a system of general propositions, but a Man, and a particularized man, our creed being consequently a recital of particulars. If we take the stress on the high value of the individual out of the Gospel, we make nonsense of its call to and offer of salvation; and if we take it out of the history of Christendom, we leave unexplained some of the largest reforms in those moving centuries.

In a general theism the individual is precious because he is accountable to God and survives to render the account and receive the judgement. If he were accountable only to his fellows, whether these be taken singly or collectively, he would have no inviolable preciousness; his value would consist entirely in his service to others. The religious reference roots his value outside society, and that is why society is under obligation to respect it, even when to do so happens to be socially inconvenient. I can read no meaning into a doctrine of inviolable natural rights that does not give them a supernatural ground.

In Christian theism the preciousness of the individual has a further source. It springs not only from his accountability, but also, and more strikingly, from the Fatherhood of God. We are His *children*, or (except on the doctrine of arbitrary election) may become His children. The metaphor is a staggering one, but Christianity stands by the requirement that it be taken seriously. It means that we have, besides an affinity of nature with God (i.e., our spirituality) given in our creation, a relation of peculiar personal intimacy with Him, the gift of grace, open to all though not all appropriate it. Through this relation we are bound more tightly to one another, the supernatural bond reinforcing the bond of natural sociality, refining this, removing its limits of race, class and suchlike. Beings of such a kind cannot properly be made mere tools of, whether by a despot or by a democracy, by the domination of one or the domination of many. Those who are aware of that higher bond will serve one another spontaneously; they will not exempt themselves from the political coercions to obedience that are necessitated by the weaknesses of human nature regenerate as well as unregenerate; but they will not allow themselves, nor passively allow others, even those who are unaware of that bond, to be handled as the mere instruments of the natural ends of natural groups. Besides our earthly citizenship, we have a heavenly one—which is not an excuse for rejecting the lower, but the paramount reason for raising it.

If this third article looks like individualism, some will object that in these enlightened days we have scrapped individualism for collectivism. We have. Is that, however, the slightest reason why an expositor of the Faith should pipe to the current ditty? But it is not individualism. It is not the plainly false proposition that society consists of atoms, which are only casually together, having no essential interdependence; or the silly proposition that everybody should be allowed to do as he pleases. It does not say that society exists for me, but for me *and all other me's*. It does not say that my society—my country, for example—has no strong claims[1] on me; it says that such claims are not my only obligations, and are not always the paramount ones. Further, in Christian theism it is accompanied by another doctrine which, taking for granted our natural sociableness, requires this to be lifted to the more intensely social level of 'love', so turning society into a brotherhood. Christianity is a deeply social religion. It makes us 'members' (organs or limbs) of one another, though not members in that sense of the State. It is against collectivism only if this works by hate, or by contracting love to one's fellow-collectivists, or if it treats a group as having ends that override all the ends of all the members, or if it conceives welfare chiefly in material terms, or seeks it by organizations so ponderous that they

[1] What they are is not specified in the Gospels; they are relative to circumstance, and are left to conscience and gumption, on the assumption that Christians will keep these quick and moving. 'Give to Caesar the things that are Caesar's' can only perversely be read to mean that we are to do what *any* Caesar—a Nero, a Hitler, a Politburo—demands so long as he does not interfere with our devotions.

require a disproportionate amount of our attention. With collectivism understood as an economic technique alternative to capitalism—assuming that we must have the one or the other, for we are now well schooled to think in two's—the theological interpretation of society is not directly concerned, except in so far as it may carry with it any of the consequences just mentioned.

The theological doctrine of society could doubtless be carried further, but the above is enough to indicate its nature, its continuing relevance, and its teaching possibilities. Alongside it could be set the biblical doctrine of society, the exposition of relevant texts in the Old Testament and the New. There is also the social teaching of the medieval Church, of the Reformers, and of some of the Christian teachers of the nineteenth and twentieth centuries. The study of these, however, involves much scholarship, and is therefore not well suited for general teaching. I am sure that the theological doctrine is the most useful: it is not expressed in terms of past historical situations; it is immensely suggestive and powerfully impelling, evoking ideas, guiding judgement, and imparting action-producing motives; and it is the most teachable, being susceptible of both simple and progressively elaborate statement, and therefore adjustable to every level and sort of adult mind, if that mind be religious.

THREE

THE ETHICAL DOCTRINE OF SOCIETY

A CHRISTIAN cannot, in his Christian aspect, sharply separate theology and ethics, his religion and his morality. But it is useful to consider morality in its own terms. The working out of a theory of *social* ethics is one of the most urgent needs of our day. It would be too much to say that the lack of one is what is responsible for the present drifting and clashing of societies national and intra-national, since there is wickedness at work as well as ignorance; but there are many people who are looking for moral guidance in matters of social policy and action, and they are not getting it, and therefore, perplexed to the point of paralysis, they are not able to supply that stability at the lower levels, and that minor leadership, which would at least put some brake on society's blind and gigantic jerks, and might—if the ancient influence of minorities has not been finally destroyed by the new power of mass-control—give it a turn in a right direction. While there is much truth in saying that these are days of an unparalleled awakening of the social conscience, the conscience is rather a discontent with the actual than a vision of the principles and ways of better social living, and is therefore erupting into hasty and unconsidered action that is probably creating more difficulties than it is removing. For example, discontent quickly flames into hate, and hate is not a good instrument of reform. Conscience as a steady imagination of finer social possibilities is formed only through long reflection, and we are not being taught how to reflect on this most complex sphere of experience. We have inherited very little in the way of social ethics.

If this last sentence be doubted, ask what books, what

authorities, we are to turn to for either theoretical or practical answers to the following questions: (a) How should a *group* behave? Substitute for the very general term 'group' such terms as trade union, government, nation, and the United Nations Organization, and the question becomes sharply topical. What principles should govern *their* action? (b) How should an individual behave when acting as a *member of a group*, for example, as a citizen, or as a member of a trade union voting on a motion to strike? Should a man marrying late, used to giving freely to good causes, no one suffering but himself, let these causes down when he becomes responsible for a household? (c) How should an individual behave when acting as a *representative of a group*? Think of those who have to negotiate a dispute about wages or working conditions, or of the officials of a political party, or of a Member of Parliament, who has the embarrassment of representing three groups, his constituency, his party, and his country. Is each to act entirely and only in accordance with his private conscience, demanding nothing that he would not demand for himself, and always conceding what he would concede on his own account?

These are the questions that constitute social ethics— those that arise out of the existence—the rightful existence —of groups, and out of the solidarity that is in some degree essential to the existence of a group. They are the very questions that most bother us today. The usual ethics— Greek, Roman, and Christian—have thrown very little light on them. In consequence, the very authority of moral judgement is being supposed in many quarters to be shaken, and what are called 'realistic', i.e. non-moral or immoral, solutions are being sought. It is quite generally not noticed that the several usual ethics have to do chiefly with conduct in its individual reference—that is, with how a person should behave with regard to himself and with regard to others in their individual capacity. Most of us know the principles of that sort of conduct, our defect being a lack of sagacity or of grit in carrying them out. But the very principles of the other sort of conduct have not been opened to us; indeed, the possibility that behaviour that has only individuals in mind and behaviour that has groups (in their group-unity) in mind might be *morally* governed by somewhat different sets of principles has rarely been seriously examined. Having only the ethics of individual action to work with, we have either proceeded blindly in fields which it cannot cover, or else have supposed that what it cannot cover must thereby be outside the province of moral control. We are now reaping the consequences of both suppositions, the stupidities of the first and the immoralities of the second.

Since there are in fact two kinds of human units, invididuals and groups, we might reasonably expect that conduct that has only the former in view and conduct that has the latter in view will require for their guidance two different sets of principles, even if these should not turn out to be wholly or ultimately different. Or, starting from experience, the failure of individual ethics, with which alone we do virtually all our moral deliberation, to guide us through our contemporary labyrinth, should itself suggest that we must think out an additional set of moral principles applicable to group-conduct; and all the more so because the area of strictly individual action, i.e. individual in aim and not only in origin, is being heavily reduced (though it may well be that the reduction can be carried to a point where not a more adequate morality is called for, but where nearly all moral action becomes impossible).

In short, there is room for two sorts of ethics, one individual and the other social, the latter comprising three branches, dealing respectively with the right and wrong of group-action, membership-action, and representative action. Although all action is carried out by individuals, there are these four types of it, and we need light on all four.

Our trouble as Christians is that the New Testament has virtually nothing to say, at any rate overtly, on the problems arising out of the existence of groups. Here and there a text may be adduced, but either it must be given a forced exposition or we find it unilluminating for current practice. Why are our foundation-documents so silent on the issues that dominate our life today? One reason should be obvious, namely, that in the days when they were written—and presumably they were written to be intelligible to the people then living—there were not the many firmly organized and influential groups that mark contemporary society. There was, it is true, a State then as now, but it was ruled from above, so that citizenship meant obedience, not responsibility as we understand it. Our Lord spoke to mere subjects, and Paul wrote to mere subjects, even when he wrote to the Romans. This historical explanation of the silence of the New Testament on the matters that are now gravelling us may not be thought adequate by theologians, but it is so plain and certain an explanation that it must not be obscured. Whatever permanence there may be in the hearts of men, we of the present live in a world that has very different social structures and classes from the world of New Testament times, and the new conditions have set us new perplexities because the principles enunciated for the old days have no obvious or direct application for the present days. The New Testament has a theology of society, and it has an ethic of individual action, but it has no overt social ethic.[1]

[1] I am ignoring the Old Testament, partly for the sake of brevity, and partly because of recent changes in the study of it which I have not been trained to follow.

How, then, are we to begin to work toward a Christian social ethic? Some Christians are so tied to the New Testament that in respect of matters where it does not directly help they are inclined to fold—or throw up—their hands and wait for the dreadful apocalypse. But has God given us nothing but that matchless book? Have we not eyes and ears and other sources of experience, and memory to hold experience, and brains to examine the gathered experience, and conscience withal to judge it? Presumably God gave us these that we might use them. But these are all totally depraved? So we are being told in certain quarters. The declaration seems to me to be an evident error of fact, and a libel even on the unregenerate —that is, if it is intended as more than an abstract theological theory invented to overprove man's need of redemption. Further, Christians have, or should have, a Christianized conscience, and, so far as they have, it would be wicked not to exercise and trust it over the whole field of experience. Finally (though it is implicit in the last point), if we may remind ourselves in practice of what we usually remember only in theory, we have, or ought to have, the guidance of the Holy Spirit, and we have this, or may have it, both as individuals and in the fellowship of the Church. All which are arguments, the usual arguments (I have cribbed the lot from open sources) against bibliolatry. They can be perversely used as an excuse for leaving the Bible alone. They are here intended to show that the Bible is not surrounded by a vacuum, but is continuous with other supernatural agencies, and with natural ones. We are provided for very richly, and should use our riches.

At this point it may be helpful to give a few illustrations of the difficulties and confusions that we fall into in social judgement because of our habit of thinking in terms of a purely individual ethic.

Consider first one of the deepest sources of the recent clashes between Britain and Germany. Britons have been brought up to believe that the actions of a nation are subject to the same moral laws as the actions of a private person. The Germans have been habituated to believe that the moral laws of State action are quite different from those of individual action. The last two wars were *not* merely games of power-politics; they were also, and tragically in the proper sense of this term, the clash of two different moral mentalities. The German theory, I shall assume, has been disproved by the awful shock which its practical consequences have given. What we must not do is to infer that the disproof of the German theory establishes the English one. The latter, if it is to stand, must be established independently. Now we, like all other peoples, believe that the State may rightly do what the individual may not rightly do, e.g. that it may take people's money away whether they want to give it or no (in taxation), and that it may deprive wrongdoers of estate and liberty. If we are right in these particular beliefs, we are wrong in our general theory. Neither the British theory, then, nor the German one can stand alone, though each contains some truth; which suggests that not only is there one set of moral principles for State action and another set for individual action, but also that the two sets *overlap*. Here is a possibility, a hypothesis, which deserves to be worked out and tested.

Take a related problem, that of collective responsibility, which may again be illustrated from the two wars. Many Britons have held that the German people, not its Government only, must be held responsible at least for the way in which the wars were waged, if not also for initiating them. With the truth or falsity of this view we are not here concerned, but only with the assumption in it that a nation can be held guilty. Other Britons have retorted that 'you can't indict a nation' (though some of them have indicted the British for indicting the Germans, which is a proof that they have not understood their own principle). Here is a clash of principle: on the one hand, a whole people can be blamed (or praised); on the other hand, we can be blamed only one by one, each for his own attitudes, commissions, and omissions only. Which is the right principle?

Although I set out only to illustrate, this is too interesting a question to drop. Let us see where the second principle leads us. The League of Nations, and its successor, the United Nations Organization, were devised to put a stop to the international disorder of which war is the grossest expression; as individuals are put under superior restraint, it was argued, so too must the nations be. But what meaning is left in this arguing if each nation is not to be regarded as a whole? An international morality requires nations to be the moral units. If we substitute governments for nations, we make the scheme both morally queer and unworkable in practice, for we should be implying that each government is responsible not to its people, but to the international body. Such a separation of government and nation would be no guarantee of peace, nor would it allow of any rectifying justice after war. Suppose that a government commits aggression against another country, overruns it, and exploits it economically. This would scarcely be possible without some backing from the nation, which also would benefit from the loot. How *could* an international tribunal correct the injustice in a way that would penalize only the government? And *ought* this to be its aim? The principle that a nation cannot be a unit of moral responsibility is, logically, a denial that there is such a thing as national responsibility, and in application would be more likely to lessen international morality than to promote it.

Conversely, if we are convinced that we must have an international tribunal, we are committed to treating each nation as a unit. We cannot have it both ways.

The objection to the principle of national responsibility is, of course, that it requires us to hold responsible for the action of a nation even those of its members who could be proved not to be responsible for it. It needs no thought to see that this principle, so expressed, is absurd. The objection is as plain as a pikestaff. Quite; and this very fact makes it suspect—*it needs no thought.* Is this how one of the most agonizing problems of our day is to be solved? Surely there is a confusion of thought here. When we are making that objection we are thinking by habit in terms of a purely individual ethic, and are assuming that no other sort of ethic is possible. The assumption does not answer the question, but merely begs it. It simply ignores, or fails to see any moral significance in, the fact that, besides being related as individuals to individuals, we exist in firmly organized groups that function, and must function, as wholes or units. If all responsibility is individual responsibility, all morality is individual morality. If this be so, in order to secure morality either we must abolish all firm groups or else every individual must be completely free to quit them whenever he disagrees with them. In either case we should have individualism with a vengeance, the collapse of our political institutions and of so much of our justice, economy, and culture as needs the protection and support of the State. We must choose between having nothing but individual responsibility with no organized solidarities, and having, in addition to our realm of personal freedom, organized solidarities with collective responsibility. Again, we cannot have it both ways

If we recognize that we—certainly we in this country—have been trained to think morally in terms of an individual ethic, we shall give up blindly pressing its terms when we are thinking of groups; and if we admit that the moral relations of groups are not likely to be identical with those of individuals, since groups *can* do what individuals *cannot* do and since obligation is relative to power, we shall begin to think *also* in terms of a social ethic. We shall then see that there are two kinds of responsibility, both of them moral and yet each differing from the other importantly. The recognition of this difference will enable us to remove the apparent absurdity mentioned in the preceding paragraph. We can now say, in respect of, for example, a national crime, that a given individual is innocent from the point of view of individual ethics, and yet partly guilty from the point of view of social ethics. Between these two judgements there is no contradiction. The one fact is simultaneously judged by two standards. The first standard has to be affirmed against those who would obliterate the person in the group, the other against those who squeal or rave when they are co-involved with the rest of the members of their nation (or other group) in the consequences, natural or penal or both, of the nation's folly or crime. No man, says the first standard, can be acquitted of responsibility for his own actions; no man, says the second standard, can be so loose a member of certain groups that he may contract out of them at will in order to exempt himself from the common lot when this is a painful consequence of his group's misdeeds. The first standard is a rebuke on abjectness, on complete surrender of judgement to the group, the second on proud or peevish forms of individualism. The first is the moral safeguard of the individual's individuality, the second the moral safeguard of the group's integrity.

This notion of collective responsibility is thus a necessary postulate if we are to be able to treat groups as moral units, if we are to regard a group's actions as subject to a moral rule of right and wrong; and it is the special basis of moral judgement on an individual so far as he is acting in his capacity as a member or as a representative of a group, saving us from the cruel narrowness of judging a man so acting by precisely the same standards as we would a man acting in the full freedom of his private capacity upon others in their private capacity.

I have not considered in this connexion our solidarity in sin, which is surely as much a fact of experience as a doctrine of Christian theology. Sin takes us beyond ethics, to which in this chapter I am confining myself. I am not at all sure that all that I have said above holds of it. So far as each of us has contributed something sinful to society—and each of us certainly has—each of us is individually responsible for society's consequent sins. We cannot go on to say that each of us is responsible for all society's sins; and I have the gravest doubts about saying that we have a collective responsibility for these, since for anything that is correctly called sin our responsibility is not indirectly but directly to God, and God, I assume, judges us one by one.

Finally, in some such way we may bring clarity and charity into our judgement on the actions of men acting in a representative capacity. There has always been, and presumably always will be, action of this sort, so that a study of it ought to be given room in the general theory of ethics. In a democracy such sort of action is very greatly extended, both in scope and in the number of individuals committed to it—democracy in one of its aspects being the multiplication of representatives—so that right judgement about it there becomes a matter of constant and immense importance. Popular conversation about a town council-lor or a politician, and newspaper comment on such persons, are a depressing enough proof of our confusion and cruelty in this matter, and it is in the light of it that we must understand the increasing flight from public office of sensitive, serious, and trained men, reluctant to expose themselves to the fickle and easy obloquies of the newspaper column, the club, the 'pub', and the drawing-room.

So far as a man is a representative, he is not himself. His scope and power of action may be enlarged, but his private discretion is reduced. He is not fulfilling his office, but either neglecting or exploiting it—both alternatives morally shocking—if in it he acts in precisely the same way as he does in his private relations. If I may overstate in order to make my point stand out, he is responsible not to his own conscience, but to that of the group he represents. Having accepted a charge, he is under obligation to carry it out so long as he is in office. It makes him responsible both for the group and to it. He has therefore to serve *its* interests, and in such ways and by such standards as *it* is prepared, in general, to approve. This is surely the proper sense of representation, the adoption of which is one of the typical marks of democracy. We could draw the distinction between a representative who is merely a delegate and one who is something more, the former being under specific orders and the latter entrusted with a general charge; but the distinction, however important in practice (as Burke saw, declining to allow election to Parliament as delegation), is in our present context one of degree rather than of kind.

Of course, a representative is not only, wholly, always, a representative. He is a private person as well. It is this very doubleness that sets the problem. He has a conscience of his own, and he has undertaken to be the organ of the conscience of the group. The former commits him to almost unlimited obligations, while the latter narrows them; and in respect of method the former is likely to have more and firmer scruples than the latter. By the former he has to seek the interests of others, whoever they are (at any rate, if he is a Christian); by the latter he is tied to seeking the interests of his group. On the one hand there is the pull to a general altruism, on the other the command to promote a group-egoism. If the two consciences could be made utterly distinct, there might be no difficulty. But they cannot. The private man survives in the representative; he is one mind, not two. His personal conscience, if it is at all developed, will not abdicate completely when he is acting representatively. Yet it cannot then rule alone, since if it did he would be wholly himself and thereby not a representative. He is under two sets of obligations, which cannot be sharply separated either in thought or in practice.

Sometimes the two consciences, the two sets of obligations, will clash so sharply that the one or the other has to give way. Suppose that the representative finds himself about to be committed to a policy or action that so deeply revolts his private conscience that he has to refuse to do his representative duty. In that event another representative duty arises, namely, to offer his resignation.[2] The case is ethically interesting because it indicates that in some clashes the last word rightly belongs to the private conscience. There are some things, most of us are sure, which no man should do even representatively. We might disagree what those things are, but what each man honestly and after due reflection thinks to be such he is bound to refrain from. There are occasions, then, on which even in the representative the private conscience has the supremacy. But has it on *all* occasions of conflict? This is the question that forms the core of the ethics of

[2] His group has an alternative to accepting this. It may appoint someone else to act for him—if rules and the circumstances allow of this, if the issue is a particular one, and if the group holds him in high regard either generally or for his scruple in the particular case.

D

representative action. The answer, it seems to me, is No, for if every representative took his bat home and refused to play every time he found the requirements of his group at variance with the requirements of his personal conscience, the world's business could not be carried on, unless only those persons were appointed to public posts who have little or no private conscience, and then the world's business would be carried on at a heavy moral cost.[3] Once more we encounter a common human problem for which the ethics of individual conduct alone makes no clear provision. Representation, it seems, creates another order of obligations, which are not merely legal or conventional but genuinely moral, and which *sometimes* are to be given precedence over the other order. When? The question demands an answer, and so far as I am aware the answer has not been worked out at the level of principle.

What is to be said on the above matters from the Christian point of view? The Christian ethic is, of course, social in a very real sense. It puts our sociality in the very forefront: to the social impulses and needs which we have by nature (and which are therefore the gift of God as Creator, as a part of His natural providence) it adds the higher principle of 'love'. Nevertheless, this supernatural bond is between individuals as individuals. True, the Christian ethic exalts the family, making this the ideal type of society, and beckoning us all to enter the one family of God; and the family is a group, and the tightest of all groups. But what makes it the Christian type is its being the one group in which all relations are

---

[3] A pacifist statesman could not and would not become Minister of Defence. But must a Christian Prime Minister resign if his office obliges him to do or authorize to be done something that is not Christian? Was he appointed *because* he was a Christian and *in order to* carry out a strictly Christian policy? Should a teetotal magistrate refuse to have anything to do with the licensing laws?

personal, governed by the uncalculating mutuality of natural love. All other groups are governed by a common end or purpose, and by rules framed to safeguard that purpose. For these groups the Christian ethic does not explicitly provide. One reason for this has already been given—that at the time when that ethic was promulgated such groups were few, and less dominant over every individual than they are today. Another reason may now be brought out quite starkly—that the Christian ethic, taken in its strictest sense as the prescription of the life of 'love', is not a complete ethic. It is an ethic of grace, of life supernaturally supported, marking out the way of the redeemed and the sanctified. It presupposes a natural ethic, an ethic of the best life for the unredeemed, and for the redeemed when they are prosy, tired, or hemmed in by circumstances that give 'love' no right of way. This lower, yet high and hard, system of natural morality is referred to and at times apparently sanctioned in occasional sayings and parables of the Gospels and at some points in the Epistles.

This natural ethic of conscience is not to be despised, even if at our best moments we may look down on it. It is not the ethic of law and justice only; it embraces sympathy and generosity and sacrifice. It demands, and has produced, superb nobilities. As both a demand and a possibility of our nature we have to refer it to the God who made that nature. Indeed, it is one of the aspects of our nature that send arguing thought, apart from revelation, up to God. Further, it is a standing warning or safeguard against that perversion of the religious imagination which leads us to exempt ourselves from the common duties, especially the little ones, and the dull ones: it is a stern admonition that if we are to pretend to a better morality, this must be *at least* just and generous, above these and not below them, and extending their range beyond the common limitations. Conversely, the Christian ethic is an admonition to our natural selves that even the finest ethic of conscience falls short of both the ideal to which God in Christ has called us and the possibilities of motive and deed which are possibilities only through His grace.

I suspect that it is from the natural ethic that we shall have to derive our social ethic, if this is to be applicable to anything like our present conditions. After all, group-life is a natural need, not a supernatural one (except in the Church); and the growing organization of it is a natural consequence of growing populations and growing technical and cultural achievements. We should be conferring an unsuitable sanctity on, for example, our political parties, trade unions, industrial associations, and suchlike, and even on the State, if we supposed that the way they ought to behave, and the way we ought to behave in them, can be deduced only from Gospel principles. They are, with all their importance, relative things, of the earth earthy, springing from natural needs, shaped and reshaped to serve natural needs, and therefore are to be judged largely by the principles of the natural conscience, certainly not in every detail by the ultimates or absolutes of the religious consciousness. If so much be granted, we shall preserve ourselves from the dreadful mistake of allowing to our very relative institutions absolute value, and thereby absolute claims upon us. We shall not pretend divine authority even for the United Nations Organization or for democratic institutions, still less for particular trade disputes, and shall thereby free ourselves of the charge of trying to silence criticism of these by implying that it is either blasphemous or atheistic. The Church has been guilty in the past, and many Christians are guilty now, of casting the mantle of heaven over a transient and corrigible earthly institution or policy or programme. The term 'sacred' has been much over-worked.

This is not to say that social morality is altogether out-side the scope of distinctively Christian judgement and intervention, for, in the first place, it falls under what I have called the articles of the theological doctrine of society, and in the second place, it would inevitably be modified by the Christian attitude of 'love' (for example, by pushing farther and farther away or blurring the boundaries which the ordinary conscience draws rather tightly round our social obligations). What I am arguing is that a social ethic must be worked out *first* on the basis of the natural conscience, and *then* be qualified by the deep changes which 'love' would entail. My reasons may be concentrated under two heads: (1) I cannot *deduce* from the Christian ethic a social ethic that is directly applicable to anything like our present conditions, because, as I have said repeatedly, the ethic of 'love' seems to me to be about the relations of individuals to individuals, not about relations that involve organized groups. Nor can I *picture* a perfectly Christian society—neither a utopia, a dream-community set under no real conditions of geography and history, nor any existing nation made entirely Christian: I could not give to such a vague image as I might form any *working* details, for instance, how it would produce and distribute its wealth, or manage its foreign affairs, though I could, of course, say quite confidently that this or that thing in actual society would not be in the ideal one. (2) Our world, even our nation, is not Christian. Until it is, an applicable social ethic must be a largely natural one. If at the present juncture we Christians were to go to society with nothing but principles which only Christians can believe and only Christians handle with effect, we should fail to come to grips with the special and historically conditioned difficulties of our day, and might have little but condemnation for the whole existing order. Our preaching might be right, but our practice would be unco-operative. If, on the other hand, we are to co-operate with our fellows, we must as far as we can work with principles which we may fairly expect them to honour *now*—that is, we must follow the natural conscience.

If this looks like a poor compromise, we must ask ourselves bluntly how many of us Christians have so mastered natural morality that we can afford to despise it. So far as there is compromise in the above suggestion, it is the compromise not of fear, weakness, or ambition, but of love. In any case we are, I believe, entitled, when the Christian ethic is not or not yet realizable, to follow an ethic that is compatible with the Christian ethic and preparatory to it; and such, I would maintain, the ethic of the natural conscience is. In this sentence I speak against the Barthians, and also in this corollary, that if the world will not be saved, Christians are under obligation to try to get it mended, both because 'love' prompts us to do so, and because to mend the natural order is to fulfil the natural providence of God. Of course, it is a second-best, but where this is the best achievable in the circumstances, it is practically the best. We may call it the second-best not in order to reject it, but in order to remind ourselves that it is not the ideal.

FOUR

FAITH AND FACT

ABSTRACTNESS is the bane of a great deal of current talk about society. Thinking about anything so large as the whole society of men, or of a nation, cannot, of course, avoid some abstractness, but if the thinking is to have any practical use the abstractions must be firmly anchored in facts. The present intellectual fashion tempts us to think in terms of very general concepts that have lost connexion with the content and pulse of real life, as when we ask why the *nations* can't live peaceably together, evaporating the deep dissimilarities of many peoples under that highly abstract term. Another kind of abstraction consists in thinking with only a part of one's personality, as when we think about social problems purely as Socialists, or Conservatives, or Liberals, or workers, or managers, or as Christians. In any of these capacities we tend to think too selectively, tearing some aspect or other of life out of its relevant context. One of the recurring points in the preceding chapter was that if we come to society with *nothing but* our peculiarly Christian ideas and experiences, we shall find social problems in their contemporary form baffling. We are then thinking with only a part of ourselves. For none of us is *wholly* Christian. Besides being supernaturally related to God through Christ, we live in a natural world, and have experiences and ideas naturally drawn from it, some of which seem to be very appropriate. Christian experience does not take us altogether out of this world, nor does revelation either disprove or displace all the knowledge of this world that we get through the natural channels. Some things can be learned only by hearing and seeing and by thinking about what we see and hear.

In other words, faith alone does not throw enough illumination on our present social difficulties to enable us to understand them—for it is far too easy to dismiss them all with a wave of the hand as being due to something we vaguely call wickedness, and it is wrong as well, since stupidity and ignorance are responsible too. Nor does faith alone enable us to master those difficulties in practice. Stupidity and ignorance, for instance, require to be dealt with by the educative way. Even a saintly Cabinet (and even assuming that they were governing a saintly people) would need something besides their faith; they would have to know the structure and ways of working of the nation's life—its finance, trade, transport, schools, professions, and so forth. If they did not know these, they would muff their job dreadfully. Being a Christian is no more a sufficient qualification for theorizing about a society, or ruling one, or trying to reform one, than it is for cobbling. We require a cobbler to be skilled in mending shoes; if he is in addition a Christian, we can count on further excellence in his service. This is surely the principle of Christian vocation, holding in all cases—not being simply called to a job, but learning how to do it competently. The distinctively Christian contribution is an enhancement, not a displacement, of natural knowledge and skill. A great deal of Christian preaching and teaching is at least suggesting that to get a better society it is enough for us all, rulers and ruled, simply to be more Christian. Belief in the sufficiency, the adequacy, of faith is tantamount to a repudiation of the realm of Nature—that is, of the requirements of God's natural providence. *Sola fide* belongs to the doctrine of salvation, not to the doctrine of social betterment, which is the limited theme of these chapters.

To better society we have to know it as well as the better, to know the facts of it as well as the ideal for it. Merely to want to change it is a pathetic mood; merely to see what to change it into is excellent theorizing or noble dreaming, but to act merely on the latter is to start an unconsidered revolution. The distressing space between the is and the ought can be neither jumped over by the impatient nor walked through by those who are ignorant of its geography. We cannot expect facts to fly to our principles as if these were magnets, nor can we violently impose our principles on the facts. The world has a structure of its own, a cause-effect structure, describable by saying: 'If fact A, then fact B; and if B, then C; and so on.' Therefore, to get fact Z we must first get fact Y, and X and W and so on. This set of letters in neat alphabetical order is, of course, an almost absurd simplification, but its purport will be clear—that in order to reach any state of affairs that we regard as desirable we must, by a natural necessity, work toward it from the given situation by the route (or routes, for there are usually more than one) marked out by causal laws. The knowledge of this network is clearly a condition of successful action.

In older days most folk acquired a fairly sufficient acquaintance with the causes and effects in their social surroundings in the ordinary course of experience. They were able to do so because their effective surroundings were usually very limited, and also very simple. They were not caught up in a mesh of groups, as we are; they were far less affected by remote happenings; so that they had not the practical goad that we have to bother themselves about the larger superstructures above daily living. Besides, they did not possess the political power and opportunity that we have to change those superstructures. Ordinary experience, ordinary intelligence, and the simple maxims of morality were sufficient to carry most people through their responsibilities. It is surely quite plain that they are not sufficient now—which is why millions of citizens who do have those qualifications, and only those, are feeling puzzled, frustrated, and helpless. The difficulty will not be solved by giving them saints as leaders, or even by evangelizing all of us into saintliness, since this neither is nor necessarily implies that knowledge of facts and their causal relations which is as indispensable as character for the right ordering of the world's affairs, and which in a democracy must be fairly widespread among the people. Assuming a certain social ideal to be right, we cannot realize it until we have studied the various causal ways to it, and cannot realize it well unless we examine those ways to see which is (a) technically the best, that is, the most efficient, (b) morally the best—that is, the one most congenial in spirit to the moral ideal—and (c) within our power to follow.

In this respect democracies are revealing an unacknowledged weakness. They are determining affairs either by ideals without causal knowledge, or by nothing but cries of pain and anger. The people who know the least—except that they know where the shoe pinches—have the whip-hand, and they are unwittingly lashing themselves, adding to the troubles which they are trying to remove. There is a problem here, which some of the newer democracies (those created in and after 1918) have seen, and have suffered from so dreadfully that they have 'solved' it by the dreadful expedient of reversion to absolutist systems of government; and which the other democracies, having so far suffered less, are loath to acknowledge, and therefore leave unsolved. We all need instruction, and instruction of the sort that we cannot take as children. Our political leaders might have given us more than they have done, but, first, we have not shown plain signs of desiring it; secondly, we ourselves chose them; and, thirdly, we have given them no time to instruct us, for we are always aggravating their tasks. If they are to do their job, they cannot be called frequently away to the platform or the microphone to make everything clear to us. Instruction must come from elsewhere; and we must demand it.

We thus return to the need for adult education. A number of secular agencies exist to supply this, supported in part by grants from the Ministry of Education. All too few members of the Church take advantage of them. In these pages, however, our concern is with the Church's own task in this field, with that which is being done (though not always *called* adult education), and with that more which must be done if the Church corporately and its members severally are to become competent to guide our society to a better order; and what I am now tediously emphasizing is that instruction in social doctrine, whether Christian or natural, must be accompanied by some reference to facts and the laws of facts. The doctrine alone is too abstract. The man in the street, including the man in the pew, finds it 'up in the air'. It is not to him applicable. To *say* that it is applicable is to give no help. To *show* that it is applicable is to point out at least some of the rungs of the causal ladder that must be scaled in order to move from the actual to the ideal. Doing that is the only way, at the level of exposition or teaching, of getting people to see what we mean by the relevance of Christianity. For most people relevance means practicability.

Keeping to the metaphor, we may say that there are two ladders between the actual and the ideal. One is thrown down from heaven—the ladder of grace—and we can learn and follow its rungs only from its divine point of attachment downwards. This sort of learning is done in worship, prayer, and Bible-reading, and, when supplemented by hard thinking, in following out the theological doctrine of society. Speaking very broadly, it may be called the deductive way. The other ladder—the causal one—is fixed down here, and we have to follow its rungs upwards, by the inductive way, by patient observation. The first has to do with spiritual laws and spiritual power, the second with natural laws and natural forces (which include human motives). We need to use both ladders. We are using only the second when we let the facts settle our ideals. We are using only the first when we suppose that our grasp of the ideal makes an independent study of the facts unnecessary. Each has its own use. The question, for example, whether war is ever right sends us at once to moral principles, natural and Christian, although I personally believe that matters of fact soon become relevant to it; whereas the question about the causes of war sends us straightway to the study of wars in history and the present.

There is such a thing as conscience for fact as well as conscience for moral principle. How little the former is felt or used by the generality of people is proved by the enormous growth and success of propaganda. Yet we have before us in our scientists a scrupulous care in their own field in the establishment of facts. It is one of the many paradoxes of our scientific day that this aspect of science remains absent from our common culture—which suggests that science, below the higher levels, is being mistaught, that it is being taught more with a practical interest in its sensational results than with a deep admiration for the austere discipline of observation and inference which it exemplifies, and which makes it a fine piece of spiritual culture. And it is one part of the tragedy of our day that this aspect of science has not been linked closely enough with our extended idealism. The latter has been too emotional—here too poignant, there too facile—to get down to the straight study of the order of fact which it is

longing to change: obsessed with the end, it has scamped
the examination of the means. Loftiness and impatience
stalk the idealist as his very shadow. We skim the questions of fact too easily. There are instances enough among
idealistic writers and speakers, but at the level of us ordinary folk there are more, for they are daily and universal—
for example, we see or hear a report of injustice, and at
once flare up in righteous indignation, damning the
monstrous deed without troubling to check whether it was
done at all, or, if it was, whether it was done in the way
that would make it truly monstrous. The 'Letters to the
Editor' in our newspapers and weeklies provide ample
illustration of this conscience for moral principle without
conscience for fact; from which even religious periodicals
are not free. Any scheme of social education that does not
address itself to this vice—this rash, brash, unhumble, and
uncharitable moral zeal—would be a very onesided
affair. To check the allegation of evil fact is as much a
requirement of natural morality as of intellectual integrity, since it is to be fair; and is even more patently a
requirement of Christian love—fairness here, like fairness
there, consisting not in the blind excusing of one person or
institution or country in order blindly to blame another,
but in a demand for the facts of the case, or, if these be
unavailable, in suspense of judgement.

A sense for fact is requisite, then, for fair judgement on
social bodies, situations or events (as on individual ones),
as well as for effective social reform. It is to be evoked by
exhortation, by example, and by instruction that makes
frequent reference to fact; by these three; and the least of
these is the first.

My concern is with the third. I am saying that our
democracy is suffering from (among other things)
uninstructed citizenship; that most of us within the
Church are as uninstructed in social fact and the laws of

social fact as are our fellows outside; that this is one of the chief reasons of our ineffectiveness in society, of our failure to moralize and Christianize the world's business; and that therefore the Church should interest itself in securing instruction in that sphere for as many of its members as will take it. The chain of affirmation is completed by adding that where such instruction is not given by, or will not be taken from, secular agencies, the Church should itself try to provide it. To all which two objections are likely to be raised—that it is asking too much of the Church, and too much also of all but a very small proportion of its members. These objections deserve an answer, the Church being undoubtedly a heavily burdened body, and its members not being an intellectual *élite*.

Part of the answer to the first objection is that the Church has already begun to attend to this realistic side of social education. In our country the Churches severally, and also collectively through the British Council of Churches, have investigated facts, published them, issued study outlines about them, and so on. This interest, however, is confined chiefly to special officers at the various headquarters, and to a relatively small number of enthusiasts in the field. The practical obstacle to extension is, of course, the multiplicity and weight of the duties that already lie on the shoulders of the ordained ministers. To add anything more might be to put on the last straw; or, if anything is added, something must be taken away to make room for it. But whatever is taken away can, if it is not to be simply dropped, be taken up by the laity; and so too can any extras. Indeed, they must be. This is the second part of the answer. A Church that leaves everything to its ordained members is leaving large resources unused. The ascertainment and teaching of the facts of social life and of their causal laws is surely a task suited to laymen, since these are doing the world's worldly business. Here is a field for that fairly large number of laymen who are left out of the usual offices of the Church. Some of them would need to be trained, others of them could do the training. Doctrine would remain in the hands of those schooled in it, a layman's theology being usually shaky.

The other objection rests on a misunderstanding. Education in social fact does not consist in turning people into sociologists or economists. Like all other sorts of education, it has many levels, taking each mind as it is and carrying it upwards as far as it can or will go. A mind that cannot go far gets something, and to that something it is entitled. Even a most elementary knowledge of social structures, processes and laws is not despicable, except from a narrowly academic point of view. It can be given to any adult of ordinary, unbookish intelligence, since to receive it calls more for practical experience than for 'brains'. The technique for selecting and imparting it has been worked out and practised for some time by tutors in the secular adult education classes, and in the talks on citizenship that have been given during and since the war to the members of the fighting Services. If the very ABC of politics and economics is not imparted on a large scale, the gulf between the ordinary fellow at the bottom and his leaders at every level will go on widening, and then the natural consequence will be either the dropping of the pretence of democracy or a mass-revolution. Already the sense of partnership, of understanding co-operation, has almost gone. The man in the street is very properly puzzled, and pardonably resentful, when, having at last got more money, he finds that it buys less goods, and when he is told that merely getting more money will only make the trouble worse. The explanation is *very* simple, and he has a right to it. Instead, he has been mystified with magniloquent talk about the 'inflation spiral'. Fine phrases, slogans and cajolery are the instruments of demagogy; democracy works by education, which presupposes a deep respect for the ordinary man. The displacement of the latter by the former is therefore a movement away from the Christian evaluation of the individual. Democracy needs to be re-baptized in its Christian source.

The value of spreading even an elementary knowledge of social fact is not yet sufficiently realized by those who could do it or see to the doing of it. We cannot fairly excuse ourselves with the *cliché* that a little knowledge is dangerous. It is dangerous when taught by unhumble minds or learned by unhumble minds; and within the Church there ought to be fewer of these than outside. Anyhow, the little knowledge is a practical necessity. Our business being to dominate fact, to remove bad fact and instate good fact, merely to concentrate on moral principles cannot be enough. Even the simplest instruction in the laws of fact will show us why we can't get the moon by asking for it, or a better state of affairs by telling our political leaders to produce it; why, in order to get what we judge to be right, we must work through the causal conditions of it; why some desirable states of affairs are at present impossible; why the removal of some ills in the quickest or most obvious way gives rise to worse ills; and so on. The laws of fact define both the limitations and the opportunities of action. They reveal the various possibilities within which we must make our moral choices and do our moral strivings.

It has been contended by some Christian reformers that the laws of social process, unlike those of material process, are not inexorable or changeless. They were arguing chiefly against the older economists, who apparently supposed that always and everywhere an economic system cannot work well without entirely free competition. The truth seems to be that some economic links (and political ones too) are changeless and some are not. An instance of the former is the law that there cannot be a high level of consumption (a high 'standard of living') without a high level of production; of the latter, that most of us will not work harder unless we are given immediate material incentives. The distinction is an important one, but it in no way weakens the point of this chapter. We must still get to know the causal linkages that are in fact operative, of the temporary as of the permanent sort, if we are to dominate them morally.

E

FIVE

SOME SOCIAL PROBLEMS EXAMINED

SOCIAL problems are bound to be hard, because they spring from the living together, in constant interaction, of millions of people; and because all of these are different, and because all of them are ignorant (even the learned), and all fallible (even the wise), and all sinners (even the saints). The wonder is that the problems are not harder. To be impatient with them, or to come to them always in a damnatory mood, is to lack both understanding and charity, and so far to be un-Christian. A nation has to find breathing and living space for those whose skill is in their hands and those whose skill is in their brains; for those who delight in doing and those who, when they are free, prefer to think or dream; for those of trained sensibility and those of untrained; for the factory-man and the farmer; for those whose passion is to be in crowded cities and those who love the quiet spaces that have not yet been filched from Mother Nature; for the sorry casualties of misfortune, ignorance, stupidity and wickedness, and for the lucky, the decent, the upright, and even the saint. With such a medley, how could life be smooth? Now add nation to nation—East to West, black to white, peasant and potentate to democrat and deputy, the man with a loincloth and a shanty living a day at a time to the man with suits and a houseful of furniture planning his next year's holiday—add each motley nation to each differently motley nation, and the monstrous medley, one might logically infer, must be an insupportable chaos. It is not. Life happens to be greater than logic. In its diverse motions it holds together even when it pulls apart. With all its aberrations, there is in it an evident cohesion. If everything were wrong, we should have no wit to know it to be wrong. The problems are problems as much because they stand out against a background of actual normality as because they are facts that contradict our ideals. So seen, the problems are not to be hated, or cried over, but to be handled with respect as natural; and there are two sorts of people who can do this, those who honour truth of fact and those who love their fellow-men.

How are we to set about tackling such problems? From the preceding pages the following relevant points may be collected: (a) In addition to the age-old problems, those that are distinctive of our time are due to the multiplication and enlarging power of groups. The area of strictly individual moral freedom and moral power seems to have been correspondingly reduced. A new area (new at least in extent) of responsibility—that of group-action, membership-action, and representative action—is opening out, making new demands on a conscience that has been trained for the judgement of individual action. An expansion of conscience is needed to match the changed situation. (b) We cannot ignore the causal structure of social fact, since right social action consists largely in the moral use of that structure. Sometimes, indeed, a problem arises out of our knowing only a bad means to a good end; and then the discovery of another means, another causal way, might be enough to solve it. So far as the causal framework is limiting, it includes the limits set against reform by sin. One evil leads to another, and when we cannot remove the sin that produces it we have to reckon with the consequences, not plan as if they were not there. Happily, causality operates on the other side also; one good thing leads to another good thing. (c) While a Christian must in the secrecy of his own mind judge all society by Christian standards, he cannot in practice require a non-Christian society to behave as if it were Christian, though he can require it to try to live up to the natural ethic. Neither will he be allowed in his own action within a non-Christian group to insist on always doing nothing less than the ideal Christian deed. A Christian, no more than anyone else, cannot in fact live in a society on his own terms. Whether or no he has a right to do so is therefore, from an immediately practical point of view, a barren question. (d) For our guidance in judgement and action we have the power of observation and causal inference; we have natural conscience; also the super-venient insight of Christian 'love', or the revelations that come through grace; and we have the theological doctrine of society, which can be written in a variety of ways (i.e. not only as in my second chapter), and which illuminates broad tracts of experience. That is no mean equipment, and if each of us uses it, not in proud or despairing solitude, but in constant co-operation with one another, we have a fair chance of reaching more clearness of judgement and effectiveness of action than we have shown hitherto. Collaborative Christian thinking on these matters is still too restricted in scale, though most people are unaware of what is being quietly done in, for example, conferences with politicians, with employers and trade union leaders, managers and foremen and workmen, to hammer out principles realistically and facts idealistically.

My general contention might be summarized by saying that a descent upon contemporary problems with nothing but a few texts or abstract principles is not sufficient. We have to think with the whole mind, draw on all our experience and faculties, and on one another's. Further, we must trust our judgements when we have so made them, instead of waiting until we feel infallible. We Protestants, having denied infallibility to the Pope, seem to hanker after it for each of ourselves in moral affairs.

How often we refuse to walk when we have only candle-light, demanding always an arc-lamp! Yet the light would probably be bright enough if we put our candles together, and kept them trimmed.

Having said so much about method, and pleaded for a whole-minded one, I shall be expected to illustrate it in application. I shall do so without pretension, lighting my little candle and showing what a poor glimmer it gives, so proving my point that we need the combined light of many candles. Sampling a few social problems, I shall not in all cases dare to suggest solutions, but shall aim chiefly at indicating how they may be analysed in a way that brings out the difficulty which I have been empha-sizing—namely, that the sort of ethics with which we are familiar, having to do with the relation of private person to private person, is not adequate when a group is involved. I shall consider three forms of group-relation-ship—of group to group, of group to individual, and of individual to group, always meaning by 'group' a society that is formally organized, not people thrown casually together.

I. The largest and most stably organized group is the nation or State. What, then, are the morally right relations among States? How *ought* these to behave toward one another?

The first answer of the Christian conscience is that each has a right to exist, and that therefore none should try to subdue or destroy another. The Communist mind would not agree; both its theory and its practice are at variance with its present peace-propaganda. The Moslem mind would allow that 'infidel' nations may rightly be attacked, in crusades corresponding to those waged by Christians in the Middle Ages. The natural conscience, if I may speak cautiously, has no clear verdict on the matter, for the ancient classical moralists did not condemn all aggression, and the modern 'rationalists' who do are probably influenced by the Christian tradition. A Christian nation, then, is obliged by conscience to abstain from aggression, the other types only by prudence.

May a Christian nation defend itself when attacked? Self-defence is an instinct; but this does not make it *right*, and the Gospels seem to condemn it. But the Gospel is prescribing at least primarily for individuals. That the prescription must be extended to the nation cannot be merely assumed; the extension must be made or denied either by a new intuition of conscience or by argument from an old intuition. There does seem to me to be a moral difference in this matter between the individual and the nation. The first decides entirely for himself, and is prepared to take the consequences for himself. When a nation decides, at most a majority of its members are doing the deciding, and it is surely a moral requirement that they should consider whether they can conscientiously commit others to the consequences of their decision—those who don't agree, and those who are not able to agree or disagree (e.g. the children and the unborn). A group-decision has thus more moral requirements than an individual decision. An individual may sacrifice himself—his freedom or his life—in resistance or non-resistance. May a present majority in a nation sacrifice the nation, and if so (for the fact of social solidarity suggests that it may), is it to be by the passive acceptance of servitude and perhaps of cold massacre, or by bloody resistance? I leave the question open, being concerned only to guard against our fetching either resistance from instinct or non-resistance from Scripture and without more ado erecting it into an obligation upon a nation. A nation differs from an individual in composition, functions, and possible longevity. We have therefore to be ready to consider if or where its special nature lays it under special obligations or gives it special rights.

But war is the climax of antecedent behaviour. If, then, the day-to-day behaviour of nations could be covered by a social ethic, war, one would think, might be avoided. Two observations may be made here.

First, such an ethic has not, so far as I know, yet been worked out. True, if we all loved one another in the Christian way, presumably the nations would, in a metaphorical yet adequate sense, also love one another; and though they might make technical blunders resulting in very painful strains, the Christian spirit would find a peaceful way out by sacrifices that involve no servitude. That this should be the ideal among Christian nations is obvious. But the so-called Christian nations are by no means wholly Christian, and there are many nations that do not, and at present cannot (consistently with their particular religious or ideological doctrines), accept that ideal. It is this plain fact that constitutes the problem of war in its contemporary urgent aspect, and any Christian theorizing that ignores it, however excellent it may be on its own ground, is doing little to help the citizen and statesman who wants to know how to ward off war now. Until recently the Eastern nations in their foreign relations were moving with surprising speed toward Western governmental standards, but this movement has now received a check; and we have Russia and her satellites repudiating in theory as in practice all the ethics of the rest of the world. There is, then, no common social ethic. What do remain common are the rules of prudence, broken by fits of folly and transcended by occasional generosity. The reality of this last can be denied only by cynics; but in a world with so many different moralities that have only scattered points of agreement, the relations among States are at present naturally being regulated largely by prudence, and are bound to be. Christian nations cannot remain at this level; nor can they entirely leave it, unless we assume, as some seem to do (wrongly, I would hold) that prudence has no place among the Christian virtues. The question I again leave open is whether prudence has or has not a larger place among the duties of a group than among the duties of an individual.

Secondly, whatever rules, prudential or higher, may win fairly general acknowledgement, can they be safeguarded against national lapses? That is, can they be enforced? It is this question that has given rise to the idea of a world-government and a world-court. Since, it is argued, order is preserved among individuals by a superindividual authority, the State, we shall be able to preserve order among nations by setting up a supernational authority, a world-State. The inference looks logical, but is not, because it passes from one sort of reality to another: it assumes that (a) what is valid for, and (b) what causally works with, individuals, will apply equally to States, to huge and highly organized groups, each of which has an historical continuity and responsibility, holding a legacy from the past in trust for the future. To discuss (a) we should have to enter into the philosophy of law, which cannot be done in a sentence or two. On (b) we have to argue from experience, and instances of the questions to be asked are: By what fair procedures could laws binding on the whole world be initiated, debated, passed and enforced? Whether the amount of force required to police the whole world could be safely trusted to *any* body of humans. Whether a regular supply could be found of men big enough to hold in their hands the strings of the whole world's life, seeing that we have a grave dearth of men able to rule even a single country. These questions concern not what would work on paper, but what would work in practice with human nature as it now is. They arise whether the suggested government be conceived as a unitary world-State or as a federal one. Underlying them all is the question whether, States having grown, a super-State can be made. Throughout our thinking we should have to keep asking ourselves whether what we are after is only peace, which sheer strength might be able to secure, or peace along with the sort of justice that entails freedom. Are we simply seeking to save life, or to save also the qualities that justify life? Here we return from questions of fact to a question of value.

Clearly, no Christian can ignore the latter. Besides, he is bound to say that a humane peace cannot be got merely by international organization; the mental qualities that make for peace—which are *very* much more than the desire for peace—must be there to enable the organization to work. He has then to look to see if they are there, and when he looks he will note that in most countries internal politics are becoming more divisive and more bitter—the opposite trend to the one required. It may be true, but seems very unlikely, that we can and shall get peace among the nations while there is so much distrust, hate, and conflict within them. It is more probable that the present fashion of grandiose scheme-making is a mass-escape from the hard daily business of self-discipline by the individual. The largest and most poignant question of group-ethics is to this extent causally rooted in in-dividual ethics. The efforts to put the world in order must of course, go on, but they can be of little avail until they are matched by efforts to heal internal strife. The former we have to leave to statesmen, doing our duty by proxy; the latter have to be made by ourselves. Unfortunately, so many things in democracies must be done by proxies that we have begun to suppose that all things can be.

Finally, an addendum to expose a confusion that is all too common in popular discussions about international order. It is usual to define a State as a sovereign, i.e. an independent, political entity, and it is thence inferred that the world is bound to be a heap of unrelated nations as long as there are States in it. In fact, it is not; the nations are economically interdependent, and are becoming more so. A similar but stronger inference from the definition is that the world is bound to be a chaos. Again in fact it is not—unless 'chaos' is here a piece of rhetorical extravagance, and neither truth nor charity is served by using stronger terms than are necessary. There is disorder, some of it reaching the horrible degree of war, but it is limited. A surprising amount of order remains. Some of it arises out of man's natural sociability and conscience —foreigners can move about most countries not only safely, but with pleasure; some out of the agreements of corporations—a cheque drawn on a bank in London will be honoured by a bank in Chile; and some out of inter-State agreements and usages, e.g. the International Red Cross, the International Postal Union, the body of international law (much of which *is* observed, and daily), diplomatic courtesies, and many special conventions. The persistence of this wide order should not be slurred over either in our thinking or in our declamations. Neither chaos nor the unrelatedness from which it is deduced exists. There is, then, no need to get rid of utterly independent nations, since there aren't any; and we cannot sensibly demand the abolition of sovereignty, as this is usually defined, since there is no such thing in fact, but only on paper as a fiction of law. There is no unlimited power, for States, even in their aspect as power-units, limit one another, and also limit themselves by treaties, conventions, and customs. What we can work for is the further self-limitation of the State's actual freedom of

action. Unlimited power could exist only in a world-State
—which is a very grave moral objection to instituting one.

So much (or little) on the relations of States. Other
instances of how groups should act toward one another
must here be given very summarily. There are the
Churches, whether in the world or within a single country;
and political parties within a country; and trade unions
in their disputes with employers. Of these only the
Churches, being wholly Christian in aim, can be held
straitly to Christian standards; yet, because they are
groups, not exclusively to the standards of the individual
ethic of the gospel. *Should* the Churches simply sink their
differences? Only if each one's sense of theological and
historical truth, and each one's special heritage of de-
votional experience, and each one's corporate steward-
ship, be dismissed as relatively trifling. A group that
represents a cause cannot in fact, and, I submit, ought
not to, give way as readily as an individual may.

This sentence is deliberately put in general terms, to
express a principle, to cover all groups, and therefore to
cover secular as well as religious ones. Political parties,
for instance, have as the very reason of their existence the
will to press a point of view, and to oppose parties that
stand for other points of view. To condemn them would be
to imply that all disagreement and opposition of groups are
morally wrong. Even in a State of Christians there would
presumably be organized political differences, if only on
the technical ways and means of working toward an
agreed end. As for the relations of trade unions and
employers, there is here a natural clash of group-interests,
and at times a legitimate clash of group-insights. If all
this seems trite, I can only plead that there has been too
much suggestion in Christian circles that telling people to
be 'nice' and agree is a sufficient ethic for group-action—
which might lead a caricaturist to picture the leaders of a

trade union expostulating that they couldn't possibly press their claim for higher wages, and the employers charmingly reciprocating by offering still higher, and neither side being mean enough to exploit the other's generosity. There are group-interests that are morally defensible; a group may rightly press a claim (not, of course, all claims) which an individual may not. Both the interests and the ways in which they are defended are subject to moral laws; only, these, while including some that govern individual action, include others that have special reference to group-action. Some of the moral laws are common to both spheres of action—for example, the condemnation of lying propaganda, of suppression of relevant truth, of abuse, and of a *merely* oppositional attitude. Of these we have instances enough in our own country for forthright Christian attention. One of them, the biased reporting by popular newspapers of debates in the Commons, is a radical offence against democracy.

II. On the subject of the relations of groups to individuals, we may again take the State as an instance, now considering it in one of its internal aspects. The State is so strong that no individual can stand against it. All the more reason, therefore, why we should try to ensure that its behaviour toward us singly shall be determined not by its mere superiority in power, but by moral considerations. We might do well to choose one of the harder questions, that of the treatment of criminals, a question that has the further suitability of having been recently brought much before the public.

That a nation must have some public rules to live by we may here assume, and also that some of those rules must be given the status of law—that is, be formally decreed by a certain procedure and enforced with the irresistible strength of the State. When a law is broken, what *ought* the State to do with the breaker?

Forgive him? This seems at first sight to be the Christian answer. Instead of jumping at it, we should consider the following points: (*a*) Can a *nation* forgive? Only individuals can forgive, and all the individuals of a nation cannot be consulted on every criminal case. (*b*) What a nation can do is to 'let off', which is by no means the same as forgiving, this being an inner attitude and that an overt act. But a law (in the legal sense) that can be broken with impunity would be a contradiction in terms. The abolition of punishment would thus entail the abolition of law; for if law were reduced to a wish or a piece of advice, the prolonged and arduous work involved in the framing, debating, and passing of a law, and the impartial application of it to particular cases, would be pointless. Either, then, State-punishment or no law. (*c*) The Christian precept of forgiveness, as it occurs in the Gospels, is plainly addressed to individuals. The extension of it to a State would have to be argued, and the onus of proof seems to me to fall on those who would so extend it. All this is abstract, in the bad sense that it can be said and understood by someone who is ignorant of what criminal acts are in fact being committed, and on what scale; but it may clear a little ground for careful thinking —and so serious a matter deserves the tribute of thought.

The facts we are faced with are that women have their purses snatched from them, lonely old women have their heads bashed and their life's savings stolen, and little children are neglected or maltreated; that goods in short supply, even rationed foods, are stolen to feed the black market; and that there is peculation of every sort and degree. Although a community that regularly produces men who can do such things has something deeply wrong with it, this communal responsibility cannot be so magnified as in all cases to destroy individual responsibility without providing a perfect excuse for all wrongdoing. As for the saying that all crime is disease, it is an epigram, not an evidenced theory. Anyhow, if actions of the kinds mentioned were allowed unchecked, violence would be met with violence and fraud with fraud, and the moral rot would spread. As has been often noted, where State-law is inadequate, there is lynch-law. The institution of State-law has at least the prudential function of preventing such insecurity and disorder. It has also a moral function, namely, to take the redressing of injury out of the hands of the victim or his partisans, so raising it above the level of vengeance to that of justice. Vengeance is blind, sometimes missing the real offender; and immoderate, sometimes passing the plainest limits. Justice is careful first to establish the facts, then to see whether a law applies, and lastly to reach both verdict and sentence impartially; and English law lays the burden of proof on the prosecution, and the procedure of our courts surrounds the accused person with other safeguards. Law is devised to secure fairness for the alleged offender, and for the real one. No lower alternative would be morally tolerable.

The supposed higher alternative—forgiveness, or at least 'letting off'—is an unargued transposition into social ethics of a principle that is taken from individual ethics; and it seems to me evident that it could not in fact either get itself introduced or work except in a dominantly Christian society ('dominantly' because in a perfectly Christian society there would presumably be only minor slips, not gross crimes). Given the general level of human nature we now have, we seem to be tied to choosing between enforced law and private redress. The latter has been ruled out long ago: it has rightly been considered a major advance in civilization that the State has deprived the wronged individual of the liberty to rectify the wrong, allowing him only the liberty of the barest self-defence—the State thereby assuming full responsibility for redress, and being guilty of injustice if it does not discharge it. It is conceivable, perhaps, that the next great advance in this connexion will be the abolition of enforcement of law, but it would have to be preceded by an enormous general moral advance. Even so, I have a remaining doubt about forgiveness in this large social reference. When A says that he forgives B for assaulting C, I find the attitude not morally impressive, but merely cheap (unless A and C are intimately related). With this parenthetic qualification, the only person, so far as I can see, who has the right to forgive is the victim; and if he is killed, only God remains to forgive. What you and I could do is to let the offender off; which means that you and I could generously expose ourselves to the risk of being his next victims. This we might have a moral right, perhaps a moral obligation, to do if (to pick out one condition only) he is to meet only you and me. But if he is to roam freely among other people, I doubt if we have any right to expose *them* to that risk. Another obligation here enters in. In sum, we may say that State-law, watching the interests of all, exists not only to protect wrong-doers from private vengeance, but also to protect the law-abiding from being endangered by private magnanimity.

Such is State-justice. As long as crime is a large and constant fact, forgiving or letting off would be a sinking below justice, not a rising above it—for justice, besides being a subjective attitude, is an objective relationship. Christians may seek better laws and better legal procedure, and may work both for the reduction of social temptations to crime (e.g. poverty not due to idleness, high prices of common commodities, high taxation, and sexuality in entertainments, novels, and newspapers) and for the redemption of the individual; but they cannot fairly press for extreme leniency to all criminals unless they are utterly convinced (*a*) that the principle of forgiveness is just as binding on a nation (even a non-Christian one?) as on the Christian individual, and either (*b*) that consequences don't count at all when a principle is at stake or (*c*) that the consequences will not in fact be what our social experience predicts them to be.

There are Christians who take the injunction that we should love our enemies to mean that we should do more for them than for our friends; and that we should love criminals more than the law-abiding—for this is the effect when we leave the latter (including children, the elderly, and the simple) unprotected from the former. If they appeal to the Parable of the Lost Sheep, I would question their exegesis and chide them for turning a perfect picture into a blind rule, or for supposing one parable to contain the whole of the Christian ethic; and they could not complain if, following their method, I countered by adducing the Parable of the Good Samaritan, where the robbers barely come into the picture. Of course, a Christian should love a criminal whom he has or can have contact with (but not 'the criminal', an abstraction), and love this criminal when others do not; but he must love others too, not lightly risking *their* interests in his love for the former. Christian love is not the substitution of an unnatural partiality for a natural one; it is not something got by seizing on the extreme opposite of the world's morality. All this paragraph, however, is missing our question, which is not what attitude you and I should have toward criminals, but what the State should do with them. The State is the custodian of the interests of all its members. Therefore, from its point of view, when a man in the dock has been proved to have done a wicked deed, he is not the only person to be thought of, is not the only centre of moral reference. If I may venture to criticize from this same point of view the practice of English justice, I would charge it with not *requiring* the criminal to make restitution to his victim, where and so far as this is possible. And from the point of view of the Christian individual ethic there would be substance and good fruit in a Christian's forgiveness of A for robbing B if he either persuaded A to repay B or himself (alone or with others) repaid B. The love that omits this requirement is below justice, not above it.

It is within this section—on the relations of a group with its members—that we should have to consider social justice. This term is a vague one. It could be taken to include political justice—giving every citizen a fair share in the determination of national policy, the sort of share that is aimed at in democracy; and legal justice—subjecting citizens only to fair and published law fairly and openly administered. As in these affairs the big battles, in our own land, have been fought and won in the past, we now usually mean by social justice the securing by the State of an equal chance for all citizens in such matters as health, education, and earning a living. The question is, then, on what grounds can we lay on the State this obligation of ensuring equality of opportunity (not equality blankly, which makes no moral sense and is in fact impossible)? There is the moral ground that such opportunity is demanded by the natural conscience[1] (which the Christian conscience endorses), and the technical ground that such opportunity could in fact be secured for everybody, not by the free co-operation of individuals, but only by the authority of the whole nation as concentrated in the State, and by the resources of the whole nation so far as these are organizable by the State.

[1] This is not certain, for the modern secular conscience has been long and heavily fed from the Christian stream. True, equality of opportunity was demanded in the fourth century B.C. by Plato; but Plato, besides being a genius, was deeply religious.

F

If either of these grounds be denied, the obligation falls.

Although this topic is much too big for development in a mere essay, attention must be drawn to an anomaly in the contemporary scramble for social justice. For it is a scramble, hurried and unthinking, and therefore unaware of its implications. The usual way of putting the anomaly is that we are clamouring for rights without shouldering the duties that go with them. This is put correctly, and will satisfy many people. Some, however, will want it to be explained. The explanation is that we cannot pick out one or two demands of conscience and leave them standing alone. They are continuous with other demands of conscience (and of simple intelligence), and stand with these—which is the meaning of the common expression that there is a moral *order*. Moral notions and attitudes form a *system*. So too, indeed, do immoral ones. If, for instance, I allow brutality, I must allow other attitudes and actions that cohere with that. Similarly, if I demand freedom, and equality of opportunity, I cannot properly stop there: for example, I must recognize other forms of fairness, in both State dealings and the relations of individuals, and must accept all the demands on myself that are entailed by my demands on others—I must accept responsibility, and respond with reciprocity and also with spontaneous co-operation. Conscience is what shows me my own obligations, not only those of other people, what shows me the latter only being a mimic of conscience, or at any rate conscience shackled to selfishness or passion. Conscience exists to be taken in its wholeness, with its inconvenient and unfashionable demands as well as its comfortable and trumpeted ones. The trouble with the contemporary social conscience is that it is too selective, and rather too selfishly selective: it wants the advantages of social morality without the strenuous and severe conditions of it. Of course, we should be fed and doctored and educated and given work; but we are not in our work producing enough to cover the increased cost, are weakening our energies in the senseless sorts of entertainment and degrading them in others, are crowding the divorce courts, and are straining our prisons to bursting-point. All which is a moral Nemesis. Morality taken in bits and pieces does not work well. We have extended the machinery of social justice without providing for its material and moral maintenance.

Let us return to the question, *Why* social justice? Because it is right, of course. No; there isn't a bit of of-courseness about it; it is riddled with questionableness. In this questioning age we have a way of dodging the questions that count. We are credulous, not critical—as the propagandists are well aware. It is not at all self-evident that we should all be allowed freedom, that those who cannot afford to buy healing or education should be given it, that the weak should be protected from the strong and the simple from the astute, that the industrious should share with the idle or the fortunate with the unfortunate, or that good parents should have to pay for the care of the children of bad parents. Taken by themselves, these are dogmas, some of them scandalous ones. 'One man, one vote', taken by itself, is also a dogma, and plainly a silly one; any of its opposites seems more plausible, e.g. that the wise should have more political power than the unwise, the knowing than the ignorant, the virtuous than the wicked, the enterprising and the diligent than the easy-going and the lazy—indeed, the strong than the weak. Why on earth should this fellow who spends his leisure at the greyhound racing track have the same rights as that fellow who goes to evening classes, or mends his lad's or his neighbour's dog-kennel, or saves for a rainy day by doing without some things while the sun shines? Social justice is not self-evidencing; on the contrary, common-sense evidence is against it, such as that some of that sort of justice is wasteful, and some of it starkly unjust to some of society's best members, that is, those who contribute most service to it.

Those rights are not self-validating because they are fragments torn out of the whole that alone gives them their validity. The only way to make sense of them is to take them along with the view of man's nature which they presuppose, and to believe and live by this in believing them. They are not compatible with *any* view of man. For instance, they are crassly irrational if we are nothing but fleeting playthings of natural forces, thrown up by these, tossed about by them for a very little while, and then just crushed (the only sort of justness in the whole miserable business!). On this view, why shouldn't the strong enjoy their strength, and the clever their gains, and the industrious the full fruits of their efforts? And why shouldn't everybody, the weak included, try to get what he wants and by such means as are likely to be successful? There could be no check here but prudence, no room for conscience. There would be spasmodic acts of sympathy, for we are built that way, but we could have no reason for taking them seriously, beyond doing them to avoid the pain of not doing them, and no reason for deliberately extending them except so far as we could calculate selfishly on their being reciprocated.

But those rights *are* compatible with a religious view of man, and, so far as I have been able to think the matter out philosophically, with nothing else. They require such a view, and such a view requires them, and I am sure that they cannot be believed and lived by for any length of time apart from a recognition of that connexion, their only guarantee in both theory and practice. The notion of rights belonging to a man because he is a man (not because he is a good or an able man) has meaning, validity and practical power only when man is regarded as more than a product of animal generation and of history. If we believe in such rights, we are committed to a religion, and one of a high kind. And if we believe in the Christian religion, we are committed to such rights. In our secular civilization rights hang in the air, flimsy and unsecured.

III. We pass to the ethics of group-membership. The relations of individuals to groups are logically the converse of the relations of groups to individuals, so that it might seem as though nothing remains to be done beyond translating the present section into terms that are the converse of those in the preceding one. I am not at all sure that the matter is quite so easy. In any case, it is sounder to take the problems under this third heading just as they present themselves in experience, and let their connexion with the preceding problems emerge.

Patriotism falls under this third heading, and it is a good subject to practise one's moral teeth on, since it sharpens them. It used to be taken for granted. Under Communism it is tabooed, except within Russia, where it is excited in its most jingoistic forms. In some countries it is swelling, e.g. in the Middle East. In some Western countries it has declined—erupting in moments of crisis, but at other times unsure of itself and therefore weak. The weakening of it from outside by propaganda is one of the special arts of our day, developed by the Nazis and the Communists: by planned mental assault, the ground is prepared for easy conquest either by the mere marching in of an army or by Quislings. The weakening of it from inside is occurring partly through the disintegration of the sense of service, and, at an altogether different level, through moral criticism. It is this last that we must here consider.

Patriotism is not the same as nationalism, the latter being the name of an attitude or policy of a nation, the former of an attitude of an individual. It is a conscious and steady loyalty to one's nation. As such it is a form of idealism, at least in the sense of being a devotion to something outside and bigger than oneself and requiring concrete expression in both paid and voluntary work. It has come under fire from what purports to be a higher form of idealism, one that prescribes devotion to mankind in general. It is now, we are being told, out of date. Is this so? Or can patriotism vindicate itself in moral principle and practice? I shall ignore the Communist dogma that the loyalty of a 'worker' is never to his country, but only to 'workers' in all countries, since that dogma rests in part on a frank rejection of the entire Western conception of morality.

We must avoid the bad habit of begging questions by using terms in their worst sense, insinuating emotion in order to dodge straight arguing. 'My country right or wrong' is not a definition of patriotism. It is one form only of it. To seduce people into thinking that it is the only form, the whole meaning of the term, is to drag a red herring (it is too poor to be called a whale) across all thinking about the subject. We must avoid also the connected habit of covertly reducing patriotism to supporting one's nation in war. It must be defined quite simply as loyalty to one's country, and the question is whether *that* is morally right, and, if so, under what conditions. In recent years the negative answer has been heard rather more than the affirmative one. It runs thus: that conscience cannot draw national boundaries round its obligations. Which is surely true, but no argument at all against patriotism, since this is not supposed, except by those who are moved to discredit it, to mean loyalty to *nothing but* one's country. When there is a natural catastrophe—an earthquake or floods—in any land, relief is at once organized in many lands, and such action neither is nor is felt to be incompatible with patriotism. Like many others, I attend international conferences, where my being an Englishman is neither obtruded nor repudiated, since it is there at bottom irrelevant. As I write it is announced that the International Court of Justice has ruled for Norway against the United Kingdom, banning our trawlers from fishing in waters in which we have fished for generations. This is a blow to the material interests of my nation, and especially to the great fishing port in which I live. It would be simply perverse to say that the many Britons who endorse our Government's instant acceptance of the ruling are unpatriotic. Our country stands for the rule of law as well as for its material interests; and it is not the only country that does so. In both concept and fact, then, patriotism is consistent with wider loyalties—to foreigners in distress, and to supernational concerns such as law, peace, science and the applications of science, scholarship, art, morality (e.g. the white slave and drug traffics), and religion. Therefore there is room for many patriotisms, as of Britons for Britain, of French for France, and so on.

What could be put in place of patriotism? The question must be emphasized, because when we are dealing with minds we cannot simply tear something out of them. Current answers are confused, both in thought and in terminology. We may get some clearness if we analyse out the possible answers. There seem to be four. (a) Loyalty to a world-State. If this were unitary, how many of the two thousand million inhabitants of the earth are capable of feeling—really feeling and so living by—loyalty to anything so remote? If it were federal, how could the constituent parts of the federation function without local loyalties? (b) Loyalty to no group. This is the proper sense of cosmopolitanism. It is the attitude of the *déraciné*, the man with no roots of either place or kinship, the person who rambles across frontiers, finding all men interesting, usually liking most of them and giving and receiving personal services—but probably paying no taxes, and only profiting by, not sustaining by the steady discharge of an office, the public structures that now make living possible. Such a man is a bohemian, possibly a saint, but usually a bohemian. (*c*) Loyalty to Humanity. But Humanity is an abstraction, not a thing but a thought. To make it concrete we must mean all men, and then we are back at one or other of the first two possibilities. (*d*) Loyalty to God. Directly only? We are then ignoring our fellows. Also indirectly? We are then again back at one or other of the first two possibilities.

The rejection of patriotism on moral grounds—either as intrinsically bad or as incapable of being moralized far without vanishing into an utterly general loyalty— seems to me to be a typical instance of abstract idealism. With some it is part of a passion to make the avoidance of war almost the sole determinant of national and inter- national behaviour—a grave narrowing of outlook and policy. With others it is an attempt to jump many rungs of the moral ladder, to provide for our grandest needs without supplying the lowlier ones. We do need the narrower bonds as well as the wider ones; unless we have a sense of really belonging to some near association, we are robbed of a deep emotional security, which is more than satisfying, being also fruitful of service. The tragedy of having no felt roots has been displayed all too amply in the forced movements of many peoples in Europe during and since the late war. That need, moreover, is bound up with one of the conditions of moral growth and moral soundness: we have to begin with the nearer duties and work outwards. The nearer duties exercise us more than the remoter ones. More moral quality is required to get on with the folk whose awkwardnesses we know by daily experience than to feel a glow about the shadowy folk at the other side of the earth; and to *do* things for those awkward neighbours calls out more moral intelligence and grit than to send a resolution or a subscription to international headquarters in Geneva, Paris, or New York. A near loyalty demands and points to particular and concrete duties, while a remote one usually leaves us in generalities, so that to overlook the former by concentrating on the latter is to miss both the disciplines and the fruits of the moral life.

Further, the duties of an individual cannot be ranged entirely in an order of what may be called their intrinsic or impersonal importance—this virtue being more excellent than that because of its inherent quality. There is also the order involved in the question: To whom am I to show this range of duties? All persons have not an equal claim on me; my natural ethic and my Christian ethic appear to me to concur in putting my own family before other families, and my own students before the students of other teachers, giving me a determinate and settled task. Similarly, not all groups have equal claims on me; my own professional organization comes before others, and my country before other countries. Some sort of partiality is needed to specify moral relationships, and some of it follows from the bonds that are either made by blood or forged in frequent interaction. We are morally bound most to the people with whom we live. Here am I, born neither nowhere nor everywhere, but in England, reared by English hands, admitted freely to the treasury of English culture, given the English love of fairness, allowed the English liberty, protected by English strength, taken up into English Christianity—and the catalogue could be lengthened. Also, I have suffered with the English. To no other country am I such a debtor. Therefore, *morally* it claims a loyalty which no other country, or the whole world itself, can claim. So must every man say of his own country. If he cannot, let him seek another on which to concentrate, and so to realize, his moral capacities. If he is not allowed to move, or is too poor to do so, he is indeed wretched.

Once more, patriotism is not the exclusion of wider loyalties; it is the saving of them from woolly thinking and fluffy emotion by bringing to them attitudes exercised and tested in daily duties on our own doorsteps. And again it is not 'My country right or wrong', for it allows me to criticize my country, and impels me to do so when I find it neglecting its own genius, not making a moral use of its powers, losing its old mental courage, frittering away its resources on baubles or dopes, or deserting the religion that has been the chief source of its general wholesomeness of mind and life. If there are countries in which patriotism must be blind, condemn it there. There are many in which it is not encouraged to be blind—mine is one of them—and it is these very countries that initiated and remain the chief supporters of international institutions: the moral spirit, schooled by loyalty at home, has expanded naturally, finding out for itself both that 'patriotism is not enough' and that the something more is not enough without patriotism.

Yet these patriotisms sometimes clash in the form of war, and it may be argued that such clashes, though exceptional, are now so dreadful as to warrant the extirpation of all patriotism, despite its decent expressions between wars. The argument presupposes that patriotism is either the originator of wars or alone makes the waging of them possible. I have serious doubts as to whether the analysis here goes either widely or deeply enough. Russia's machinations in various countries give us present

instances of men who want to fight and do fight without
any sentiment of patriotism. However, the rooting out of
patriotism is tied to the abolition of States, and this
matter has been discussed earlier.

But patriotism requires *us* to fight? If so, it thereby
stands sufficiently condemned in the conscience of some
pacifists. Not of all. Others save patriotism by denying
that it has *that* requirement; for there certainly are
pacifists who love their country, acknowledge their
special obligation to it, and are ready to die for it in any
other way than that of taking part in war. The distinction
of these two kinds of pacifists is ethically significant.
Although both judge war to be always wrong, those of the
first kind are, I think, logically committed to the view that
groups (except perhaps all mankind, which is not yet a
group) are morally irrelevant, our duties being always to
individuals. On this I have said more than enough.
Those of the second kind do acknowledge duties to groups,
and especially to one's national group. These do, therefore, leave room for a social ethic, do admit some forms
and degrees of social solidarity and the obligations which
these imply. They can argue *within* social ethics that it is
wrong for groups to go to war, and therefore wrong for a
group to require its members to fight, and therefore wrong
for even a loyal member to respond to a call to fight. As
the conclusions are rightly drawn, it is the premiss that
has to be examined. The examination of it belongs to the
first section of this chapter, where, however, I had to leave
it incomplete, since I had no room to enter into the possible
answers to the question, *Why* is war always wrong?—e.g.
because God has forbidden it, because it can spring from
nothing but bad dispositions, because it cannot produce
a preponderance of good over evil consequences, or
because it is intrinsically, absolutely wrong, regardless of
motives and consequences. These answers, being all

serious ones, deserve to be tested. My own misgivings about pacifism as an immediate programme (as a witness or admonition, when humbly and sacrificially maintained, it rakes the heart to the very bottom) are, put barely, that (*a*) it presses an ideal requirement uncompromisingly in a very unideal situation, in particular a Christian requirement on a non-Christian country; (*b*) it assumes that enough of us have the great spiritual stature that would shame the aggressor, sure of his conquest, into dropping his bloody arms; or, alternatively, (*c*) that the values that justify life cannot be protected at the cost of taking life—here, I think, underestimating the ghastliness of mental and spiritual servitude, of which we have present examples in certain parts of the world. These statements are, of course, too sketchy, but I must draw to a close. If I were to add that I believe my own country deserves to be defended, I should be making a complex personal confession, not continuing the argument; and the confession would lack moral weight because my fighting years are finished.

www.ingramcontent.com/pod-product-compliance
Lightning Source LLC
Chambersburg PA
CBHW060424090426
42734CB00011B/2432